THE POWER OF INDIA

INDIA IS ALWAYS WINNER AND PAKISTAN IS ALWAYS LOSER

MR VIVEK KUMAR PANDEY

XpressPublishing
An imprint of Notion Press

Old No. 38, New No. 6
McNichols Road, Chetpet
Chennai - 600 031

First Published by Notion Press 2020
Copyright © MR VIVEK KUMAR PANDEY 2020
All Rights Reserved.

ISBN 978-1-64805-339-9

Contents

CHAPTER ONE

THE POWER OF INDIA

BOOK TITLE :MISSION UNSTOPPABLE
   SUBTITLE : WAR AND STRIKES
   ABOUT WRITER VIVEK KUMAR PANDEY
   vivek.jpg

MY NAME IS VIVEK KUMAR PANDEY . I WAS BORN IN 30 SEP 2002,I AM FROM SURAT GUJARAT INDIA.MY DREAM WAS TO BE GOOD WRITERS ,MY FAMILY SUPPORTED ME TO SUCCESSFUL AND I CAN DO IT MY SELF.How do I write? That is a question, I believe, that cannot be honestly answered by me. I may think I did a good job writing something when in reality it could be horrible. The reader is the one who decides the quality of my writing. I do not find writing to be natural to me and therefore find it to be a real challenge. My trick as a challenged writer is to do the best I can and know that I am happy with the final outcome. It may take a while to do my best and there may be quite a few problems I run into along the way.

When I write I come across a few problems that always tend to slow me down. Finding the right words is the hardest part. While I write, I try to picture what words will follow the writing I have already completed. I can rarely find the words I want or make my writing sound the way I would like it to. When I first started writing my main problem was, and still is, writer's block. I've learned to overcome that by coming up with every way I can to say what is in my head and put it on paper. It may not always work how I would like it to but it allows me to state my mind to the best of my abilities. In the end it is all about getting what is in your head onto the paper. That is one of the main factors that can affect my opinion of my writing. how to i am become a writer ,there is support of my family and teachers now i am become a writer.my fav sports is cricket and i like summer season etc.in class 5th i started writing like poem and story other.you can do everything and do it 's your self."THOSE WHO TRY NEVER GIVE UP".

In order for me to have a good opinion of my writing I have to like what I am writing about. If I am not interested in the topic I am writing about I will get bored of it and my disinterest will be obvious in the end result. I enjoy being able to state my opinion and write how I feel. My best work is on a topic I enjoy and includes what I think and feel about it. From past and recent experiences I have learned that I am more proud of work I have enjoyed writing and researching for. In the past I have enjoyed writing short stories and assignments on subjects that intrigue me or are on some of my personal interests. In the end I believe it my self............

CH 1 STRIKES

The Inside Story of India's 2016 'Surgical Strikes'

The never-before-told details of what went into India's "surgical strikes" against Pakistan-based militants in late-2016.

By **Nitin A. Gokhale**

September 23, 2017

The Inside Story of India’s 2016 ‘Surgical Strikes’

Indian army soldiers stand guard on a street on the outskirts of Srinagar, India, September 21, 2016.

The following is an excerpt from Nitin A. Gokhale's new book, Securing India the Modi Way: Pathankot, Surgical Strikes and More. It is published here with permission from Bloomsbury Publishing India.

For Col H and Col K (names withheld), the moment of reckoning arrived on the afternoon of 18 September 2016. Throughout that morning, the Commanding Officers (COs) of two separate Para (Special Forces) battalions were like most of their colleagues posted in Kashmir Valley, following the increasingly grim news coming out of Uri, the garrison town not very far from Srinagar. Well-trained and well-informed terrorists of the Lashkar-e-Toiba (LeT) had infiltrated across the Line of Control (LoC) and attacked an administrative camp in the 12 Brigade HQ located in Uri with deadly effect. At least 19 soldiers of 6 Bihar battalion, camping in tents — days before they were to take their assigned positions along the LoC — were killed in the early morning attack. Majority of the soldiers died in their sleep, resting as they were in highly inflammable tents. Although all the four terrorists were neutralised eventually, they had set off a chain of events that would culminate on the morning of 29 September.

In Udhampur, Northern Army Commander Lt Gen DS Hooda was distressed. He had been the GOC-in-C for over two years and witnessed his share of successes and setbacks as the head of India's most active Army command. Nevertheless, this was possibly the worst moment of his long and distinguished career, spent fighting insurgencies and terrorism in the north-east as well as Jammu & Kashmir. "It was terrible. Very difficult to justify what happened.

There were definitely lapses on our part," Hooda says in retrospect.

But an Army Commander doesn't have the luxury of wallowing in his own state of mind. He has to set an example by leading from the front. As he accompanied Army Chief Gen Dalbir Singh to Uri, Hooda knew the time had come to implement a plan, the seeds of which had vaguely taken shape in his mind some fifteen months ago. Even Gen Dalbir, aware of how the Prime Minister's mind worked, was thinking of something different.

Gen Dalbir was drawing on his experience during the cross-border raid in Myanmar more than a year previously when the PM had quietly authorised the strike against north-east militants holed up in the jungles of Manipur-Myanmar border after killing 18 Indian soldiers. Gen Dalbir had a hunch then that the Prime Minister may demand a Myanmar-like action if push came to shove in J&K. Cut to mid-June in 2015. In June 2015, it was under his watch as Army Chief that the soldiers of a Para SF unit of the Indian Army, based in the north-east, had carried out a precise attack on an NSCN (K) camp located inside Myanmar and eliminated at least 60 insurgents in the process. While the cross-border raid inside Myanmar was making waves and dividing opinion (see separate chapter), discussions in TV studios in India centred around the possibility of similar raids against Pakistan. Minister of State of Information & Broadcasting, Rajyavardhan Rathore told TV anchors that the option of cross-border raids against Pakistan are a possibility. He also told Indian Express in June 2015: "This is a message for all countries, including Pakistan, and groups harbouring terror intent towards India. A terrorist is a terrorist and has no other identity. We will strike when we want to."

The success of Myanmar operations had planted the seed of thought about a surgical strike in Pakistan in everyone's mind. Once during his visit to the Northern Command, then Defence Minister Manohar Parrikar too had exhorted top commanders to be prepared for every eventuality. "Although I didn't spell it out explicitly, I knew some day a grave provocation by Pakistan may require a Myanmar-like operation. So I told the Army Chief and his senior commanders to look at every possible response," Parrikar recalls. On his part, Lt Gen Hooda called the two COs (Col H and Col K) and told them that they needed to start looking at targets across the LoC, although frankly at that point in time (June 2015) neither Gen Dalbir, nor Lt Gen Hooda or the political leadership would have thought of such an eventuality arising. Till then, the thinking at the highest levels of India's political and military leadership was any major trans-LoC strike would be deemed escalatory. Remember, in Kargil, the Vajpayee government had imposed the strict restriction of NOT crossing the LoC in spite of a grave provocation.

"I thought to myself, if tomorrow someone asks us to go, how can I, as Northern Army Commander say we are not prepared?" Hooda remembers thinking. Gen Dalbir says: "From my experience in planning and executing the Myanmar raids, I wanted my commanders to make sure that any cross-border raid should be carried out with minimum casualties. My instructions were, not one single soldier should be left behind in enemy territory even if we suffered any setback." Hence, in the immediate aftermath of the Myanmar operation, the two COs were told to seriously plan to hit targets inside PoK. Other senior officers in Northern Command's planning staff also held discussions a couple of times with the MO (Military Operations Directorate at the Army HQ). They identified targets, looking for more intelligence inputs on them, and consolidating a thought process in the presence of the Army Chief and the Northern Army Commander.

But were not cross-border raids carried out earlier too, I asked Gen Dalbir. "Yes, they were," he agreed "but most actions taken in our younger days were, what we call, BAT (Border Action Team) raids on specific post(s) as retribution for something that the Pakistan Army troops would have carried out on our position(s)," he said. "What we were now planning for was much larger with greater ramifications," he explained.

ADVERTISING

For two months in the winter of 2015, the two battalions trained as whole units after years of operating in small, agile teams against terrorists in J&K. This training was to prove crucial in sharpening the set of skills needed for raids across the LoC.

In a way, it was like revisiting their basic tenets for the Special Forces men. And they loved it. Although no one could have anticipated that they would be called in to strike across the LoC, the very thought of crossing a line that was seen as taboo motivated the troops further. Indeed for over two decades no one at the highest political level had ever expressed willingness to sanction, or had demanded such an action inside PoK for the fear of escalation.

"The two to two-and-a-half months that these boys spent together helped them hone their skills in surveying targets, mount surveillance, practising infiltration and exfiltration, which in the final analysis helped them achieve what was asked of them," a senior officer in MO Directorate, privy to the development now agrees, looking back at that decision. As a result of the reorientation, by the time the summer of 2016 arrived, the two battalions had added an extra edge to their repertory of formidable skills. However, no one—not even the most imaginative scriptwriter in Bollywood — could have anticipated the events as they unfolded in September 2016.

Across the board, the langar gup (mess gossip) was full of frustration and rage. I remember speaking to some middle level officers posted in J&K in the immediate aftermath of the Uri incident. The anger was palpable. "If this is not the last straw, what is," many of them wondered aloud when the possibility of the Indian army's retaliation was discussed. NSA Doval too remembers Prime Minister Modi telling him: "This attack should not go without a response." Gen Dalbir adds: "During one of the meetings in the immediate aftermath of Uri, the Prime Minister said the retaliation should be immediate to send an unambiguous message." Parrikar, Doval and Gen Dalbir however knew they had to plan for several contingencies before attempting a Myanmar-style cross-border raid. For one, unlike on the Myanmar border, the Pakistani forces strung all along the LoC were on highest alert in the wake of the Uri attack. The terrorists would have also been told to lie low and shifted to camps located farther away from the LoC so that hitting those targets would have become harder. Moreover, no matter how remote the possibility, India had to wargame the likely escalation by Pakistan if retribution was ordered.

<u>SUBSCRIBE NEWSLETTER</u>

The week of the Uri attack was also a testing time for the Prime Minister's leadership. Modi, adept at judging the public mood, was aware that people expected him to "walk the talk" in acting tough against India's implacable enemy. Public opinion in the country was inflamed. People were calling for an all-out war against Pakistan. Even saner voices were advocating at least some demonstrable retribution. Modi was aware of the public sentiment and the anger that was building up in popular perception. He vowed immediate retribution. "I assure the nation that those behind this despicable attack will not go unpunished," he tweeted on the day of the Uri attack. Not many people took the statement at face value. After all, politicians and prime ministers in the past had pledged stern action against terrorists and their handlers many times, but had ultimately refrained from giving that final go ahead required to retaliate, urging restraint instead.

Amidst all the criticism, the Prime Minister continued to be unruffled. Recall his aides: "The PM went through with his daily routine and pre-scheduled appointments and programmes without any change, but made sure he had all possible options presented to him before giving the final go ahead (for a punitive strike against Pakistan)." All options, economic, political, and diplomatic were considered. They ranged from downgrading diplomatic ties, revisiting the provisions of the Indus Water Treaty, mobilising international opinion by furnishing proof of Pakistan's complicity in terrorist attacks, and of course punish Pakistan militarily. But he was not about to be rushed into any hasty decision. The Prime Minister however made up his mind by 23 September, five days after the Uri attack. Later that evening, he and Doval, escorted by a Major General from the MO Directorate, walked the length of the South Block Corridor from the PMO to the Army HQ Ops room around 2100 hours, much long after the corridors had been emptied and offices had closed. Already present in the room were Defence Minister Parrikar, Army Chief Gen Dalbir Singh, DGMO, Lt Gen Ranbir Singh, and a couple of MO Directorate senior functionaries. The PM sat through the briefing silently, listening with rapt attention. He was presented various options, shown targets that were planned to be hit inside PoK, and briefed on the possible retaliation/ reaction by Pakistan. Once the initial briefing was over, Modi had a couple of questions on other possible options like a precise air strike on terrorist camps, remembers a participant. Eventually, the Prime Minister agreed that a Special Forces raid across the frontier was the best possible course of action at that point, the participant added.

As one week passed after the Uri attack, the debates tapered off; people seemed resigned to live with the bitter fact that the situation in J&K and on the LoC would continue to be volatile with the Indian army unable to take any deterrent steps. Little did anyone know that India was about to unleash unprecedented and audacious cross-border strikes.

Once the political call was taken, the wheels began to move faster. In Udhampur, the Ops room was buzzing with activity. Now was the time to bring the two Corps Commanders of 15 and 16 Corps in the loop.

Accordingly, Lt Gens Satish Dua and RR Nimborhkar, heading the Srinagar-based Chinar and Nagrota-based White Knight Corps respectively, were also brought on board.

Col H and Col K meanwhile were back to their respective bases. They had much to do. Both had finalised the targets, but the men had to be selected for different tasks, although in their mind they had already earmarked some key personnel the previous winter when the entire units were training together.

As Col H remembers, "Most of our reorientation took place in the mind; we were crossing a threshold that had been embedded in the mind: thus far and no further. Now we were being asked to do a job that had not been undertaken in decades." Adds Col K: "Our boys always had the skills, but they had applied the skills to a different set of circumstances, not the task we were about to undertake. However, due to our practice and reorientation, they were at the peak of their skills." They were, like many Indian Army Officers before them posted along the LoC, aware of one-off, shallow raids launched by different infantry units into PoK. But all of them were individual punitive actions and not large-scale planned operations like the one that was being contemplated now.

The tasks were diverse. Teams had to be formed accordingly. Over the past quarter century, the Indian Army had created a strong network of intelligence operatives in the valley and within various tanzeems based in Pakistan-Occupied Kashmir (PoK). Post the Uri attack and around the time when the surgical strike was being finalised, Northern Command tapped a couple of sources in Hizbul Mujahideen, located in the general area of Anantnag, to obtain more information about the layout of Pakistani camps, and the possible routes that could be taken both to enter and exit PoK. These inputs were crucial to plan strategy and form teams for different tasks like mounting secret surveillance, raid the camps, and for guiding the troops back safely. They also had to do last minute rechecking of targets to make sure that the terrorists were still holed up there and launch pads were not emptied out after the Uri attack.

So what were the thoughts that were going through their minds as they prepared to launch the strikes, I asked the two Commanding Officers.

Looking back, with a quiet sense of pride in their eyes, both the officers recalled their state of mind: "We knew we had to hit the adversary so hard that he would be humiliated. There was no time for half-measures, no place for token gestures," recounted Col K. His colleague added: "This is what we train for: That one chance to deliver a blow so lethal that the enemy will constantly think about it when planning any misadventure."

Accordingly, the COs were told that the intent of the cross-border strikes was two-fold: inducing fear and extracting revenge. Simultaneously, total destruction of terrorist infrastructure directly opposite Uri was planned so that those who had launched the attack on 18 September would get the right message. "The idea was to let them know that we know where you are based and where you launch your attacks from and more importantly, we know where to hit you.

The message had to go up to Muzzafarabad (the capital of PoK)," Col H said, reflecting upon the week in the run up to the actual operation.

Get **first-read access** to major articles yet to be released, as well as links to thought-provoking commentaries and in-depth articles from our Asia-Pacific correspondents.

<u>SUBSCRIBE NEWSLETTER</u>

The wait was now getting shorter. It was finally over on 28 September.

That afternoon, Lt Gen Hooda signalled the launch of Operation X when he called both Col H and Col K. Separately, he wished them a simple "good luck" and told them to go ahead and complete the assigned task.

Teams surged forward by late evening, poised on the edge of the LoC, ready to cross over later that night.

Back in Delhi, Gen Dalbir briefed NSA Doval about the mission plan and worked out a mechanism to update him as and when he received inputs from the ground.

"The die was cast now. The onus was on the Army that I was leading to deliver. But I was confident of our success," Gen Dalbir recalls. Parrikar, meanwhile, was separately briefed about the roll-out of the action plan by the Army Chief.

OPERATION X

28-29 September 2016, J&K

From here onward, teams led by Col K and Col H were on their own. All of it depended on their skills, daring, ingenuity, and above all, determination to succeed in whether they would accomplish the task assigned to them.

There was no looking back now.

The operation, called Operation X in conversation but not officially named as such, was being monitored at Army HQ in Delhi, at the Northern Command HQ in Udhampur, and at Nagrota and Srinagar, the HQs of 16 and 15 Corps respectively.

As Prime Time television debates across different news channels were just about winding down, Col K's teams were making their way to the LoC. Col K, assigned to target camps south of the Pir Panjal range, led his teams across the LoC around midnight. In four hours, they were in close proximity of the objectives. Having bypassed some of the outposts close to the LoC on the Pakistani side, the teams were now truly behind enemy lines.

Barring one minor injury, Operation X had gone off with clockwork precision. Complete surprise was achieved, resulting in the higher fatalities in the camps-cum-launch pads of the Pakistanis. It also validated many conceptual plans made over the years for trans-LoC operations.

<u>SUBSCRIBE NEWSLETTER</u>

So what was the death count? I asked the two COs.

Both were candid, admitting they didn't stop to count the dead. "That was neither our remit nor the objective of the strike. We had been given a job to destroy selected targets to send a message. In light of which we performed to the best of our abilities. We can't give you exact figures. No one can, but what we saw with our eyes in those moments, tells us that we would have accounted for at least 70–75 fellows combined," both Col K and H tell me. Later that day, radio chatter from across the LoC reportedly confirmed at least 80 fatalities in the camps that were hit by Indian Special Forces.

What is Surgical Strike?

Being a soft state, India always acts or carried out harsh steps like surgical strike and Covert Operation on the basis of very specific and credible information from intelligence. India had carried out surgical strikes targeting "launch pads" for terrorists across the Line of Control (LoC) in order to justify its stand on Zero tolerance of terrorism. It is a legitimate, well planned military action intended to deal only with a specific target to avoid collateral damage.

SHAKEEL ANWAR

MAY 7, 2019 17:34 IST

What is Surgical Strike?

?

"We sleep because Soldiers are awake, we live because they die.' A set of society, which breathe and bleed nation, the army, is the only reason of our peace."

India is a soft state, but always act or carried out harsh steps like surgical strike and Covert Operation on the basis of very specific and credible information from intelligence. For example: Myanmar Covert Operation was the best example of the military's prompt and bold action when the militants ambushed an Army convoy and killed 18 soldiers in the **Chandel district of Manipur** which was the deadliest attack in two decades.

Recently, India had carried out surgical strikes targeting **"launch pads"** for terrorists across the **Line of Control (LoC)** in order to justify its stand on Zero tolerance of terrorism that never allowed terrorists to operate across the Line of Control with impunity and attack Indian citizens.

What is Surgical Strike or Operation?

The **Surgical Strike or Surgical Operation** is a military attack which is intended to damage only a legitimate military target, with no or minimal collateral damage to surrounding structures, vehicles, buildings, or the general public infrastructure and utilities. This kind of operation or strike requires intense coordination among the government, intelligence agencies and the security forces for the success. These are quick and effective strike or operation and also the reinforcement of commandos are kept on standby for any eventuality.

Top amazing facts about RAW

How Surgical Strike or Operation is followed up?

Surgical Strike

This is an act of the Armed Forces that can be followed up through raiding air, airdropping or ground strike by the team of **Special Operations (ops) Forces**. These **special-operations forces** trained enough to conduct sabotage, reconnaissance, subversive and other special operations on the territory of foreign countries during early morning hours as an **'element of surprise''**.

CH 2 OPERATION VIJAY

Annexation of Goa

(Redirected from Operation Vijay (1961))

"Invasion of Goa" redirects here. For the conquest by Portugal in 1510, see Portuguese conquest of Goa.
"Operation Vijay (1961)" redirects here. For the 1999 Indian operation, see Kargil War.
See also: Integration of Dadra and Nagar Haveli

Annexation of Goa

Date
18–19 December 1961
Location
vasco da gama

- Goa, Daman and Diu, Portuguese India
- Surrounding sea and airspace

Result

- Indian victory

Incorporation of the territories of Goa, Daman and Diu into the Republic of India

Belligerents

India

Portugal

Commanders and leaders

- India Rajendra Prasad
- India Jawaharlal Nehru
- India Maj.Gen. K. P. Candeth
- India AVM Elric Pinto
  India V.ADM Ram Dass Katari
  India V. K. Krishna Menon

- Portugal Américo Tomás
- Portugal A. D. Salazar
- Portugal M. A. Vassalo e Silva[a]
- Portugal Cunha Aragão

Strength

45,000 infantry
1 light aircraft carrier
2 cruisers
1 destroyer
8 frigates
4 minesweepers
20 Canberra medium bombers
6 Vampire fighters
6 Toofani fighter-bombers
6 Hunter multi-role aircraft
4 Mystère fighter-bombers
3,995 soldiers
200 sailors
1 frigate
3 patrol boats

Casualties and losses

22 killed[1]

- 30 killed[2]
- 57 wounded[2]
- 1 frigate disabled[2][3]
- 4,668 captured[4]

[a] Governor-General.

show

- v
- t

- e

Portuguese colonial campaigns

The **Annexation of Goa** was the process in which the Republic of India annexed the former Portuguese Indian territories of Goa, Daman and Diu, starting with the armed action carried out by the Indian Armed Forces in December 1961. In India, this action is referred as the "Liberation of Goa". In Portugal, it is referred to as the "**Invasion of Goa**". Following the end of Portuguese rule in 1961, Goa was placed under military administration headed by Kunhiraman Palat Candeth as Lieutenant Governor.[5] On 8 June 1962, military rule was replaced by civilian government when the Lieutenant Governor nominated an informal Consultative Council of 29 nominated members to assist him in the administration of the territory.[6]

The "armed action" was code named **Operation Vijay** (meaning "Victory") by the Indian Armed Forces. It involved air, sea and land strikes for over 36 hours, and was a decisive victory for India, ending 451 years of rule by Portugal over its remaining exclaves in India. The engagement lasted two days, and twenty-two Indians and thirty Portuguese were killed in the fighting.[2] The brief conflict drew a mixture of worldwide praise and condemnation. In India, the action was seen as a liberation of historically Indian territory, while Portugal viewed it as an aggression against its national soil and citizens.

Contents

Background[edit]

After India's independence from the British Empire in August 1947, Portugal continued to hold a handful of exclaves on the Indian subcontinent—the districts of Goa, Daman and Diu and Dadra and Nagar Haveli—collectively known as the *Estado da Índia*. Goa, Daman and Diu covered an area of around 1,540 square miles (4,000 km²) and held a population of 637,591.[7] The Goan diaspora was estimated at 175,000 (about 100,000 within the Indian Union, mainly in Bombay).[8] Religious distribution was 61% Hindu, 36.7% Christian (mostly Catholic) and 2.2% Muslim.[8] The economy was primarily based on agriculture, although the 1940s and 1950s saw a boom in mining—principally iron ore and some manganese.[8]

Local resistance to Portuguese rule

Main article: Goa Liberation Movement

Resistance to Portuguese rule in Goa in the 20th century was pioneered by Tristão de Bragança Cunha, a French-educated Goan engineer who founded the Goa Congress Committee in Portuguese India in 1928. Cunha released a booklet called 'Four hundred years of Foreign Rule', and a pamphlet, 'Denationalisation of Goa', intended to sensitise Goans to the oppression of Portuguese rule. Messages of solidarity were received by the Goa Congress Committee from leading figures in the Indian independence movement including Rajendra Prasad, Jawaharlal Nehru and Subhas Chandra Bose. On 12 October 1938, Cunha with other members of the Goa Congress Committee met Subhas Chandra Bose, the President of the Indian National Congress, and on his advice, opened a Branch Office of the Goa Congress Committee at 21, Dalal Street, Bombay. The Goa Congress was also made affiliate to the Indian National Congress and Cunha was selected its first President.[9]

In June 1946, Ram Manohar Lohia, an Indian Socialist leader, entered Goa on a visit to his friend, Julião Menezes, a nationalist leader, who had founded the Gomantak Praja Mandal in Bombay and edited the weekly newspaper *Gomantak*. Cunha and other leaders were also with him.[9] Ram Manohar Lohia advocated the use of non-violent Gandhian techniques to oppose the government.[10] On 18 June 1946, the Portuguese government disrupted a protest against the suspension of civil liberties in Panaji (then spelt 'Panjim') organised by Lohia, Cunha and others including Purushottam Kakodkar and Laxmikant Bhembre in defiance of a ban on public gatherings, and arrested them.[11][12] There were intermittent mass demonstrations from June to November.

In addition to non-violent protests, armed groups such as the Azad Gomantak Dal (The Free Goa Party) and the United Front of Goans conducted violent attacks aimed at weakening Portuguese rule in Goa.[13] The Indian government supported the establishment of armed groups like the Azad Gomantak Dal, giving them full financial, logistic and armament support. The armed groups acted from bases situated in Indian territory and under cover of Indian police forces. The Indian government—through these armed groups—attempted to destroy economic targets, telegraph and telephone lines, road, water and rail transport, in order to impede economic activity and create conditions for a general uprising of the population.[14] A Portuguese army officer stationed with the army in Goa, Captain Carlos Azaredo, stated in 2001 in the Portuguese newspaper *Expresso*: "To the contrary to what is being said, the most evolved guerilla warfare which our Armed Forces encountered was in Goa. I know what I'm talking about, because I also fought in Angola and in Guiné. In 1961 alone, until December, around 80 policemen died. The major part of the terrorists of Azad Gomantak Dal were not Goans. Many had fought in the British Army, under General Montgomery, against the Germans."[15]

Diplomatic efforts to resolve Goa dispute

Main article: India–Portugal relations

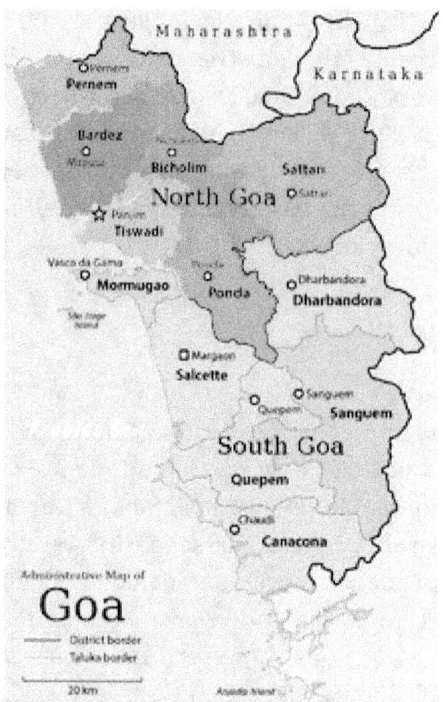

Goa, Western India

On 27 February 1950, the Government of India asked the Portuguese government to open negotiations about the future of Portuguese colonies in India.[16] Portugal asserted that its territory on the Indian subcontinent was not a colony but part of metropolitan Portugal and hence its transfer was non-negotiable, and that India had no rights to this territory because the Republic of India did not exist at the time when Goa came under Portuguese rule.[17] When the Portuguese government refused to respond to subsequent aide-mémoires in this regard, the Indian government, on 11 June 1953, withdrew its diplomatic mission from Lisbon.[18]

By 1954, the Republic of India instituted visa restrictions on travel from Goa to India which paralysed transport between Goa and other exclaves like Daman, Diu, Dadra and Nagar Haveli.[16] Meanwhile, the Indian Union of Dockers had, in 1954, instituted a boycott on shipping to Portuguese India.[19] Between 22 July and 2 August 1954, armed activists attacked and forced the surrender of Portuguese forces stationed in Dadra and Nagar Haveli.[20]

On 15 August 1955, 3000–5000 unarmed Indian activists[21] attempted to enter Goa at six locations and were violently repulsed by Portuguese police officers, resulting in the deaths of between 21[22] and 30[23] people.[24] The news of the massacre built public opinion in India against the presence of the Portuguese in Goa.[25] On 1 September 1955, India shut its consul office in Goa.[26]

In 1956, the Portuguese ambassador to France, Marcello Mathias, along with Portuguese Prime Minister António de Oliveira Salazar, argued in favour of a referendum in Goa to determine its future. This proposal was however rejected by the Ministers for Defence and Foreign Affairs. The demand for a referendum was repeated by presidential candidate General Humberto Delgado in 1957.[16]

Prime Minister Salazar, alarmed by India's hinted threats at armed action against Portugal's presence in Goa, first asked the United Kingdom to mediate, then protested through Brazil and eventually asked the United Nations Security Council to intervene.[27] Mexico offered the Indian government its influence in Latin America to bring pressure on the Portuguese to relieve tensions.[28] Meanwhile, Krishna Menon, India's defence minister and head of India's UN delegation, stated in no uncertain terms that India had not "abjured the use of force" in Goa.[27] The US ambassador to India, John Kenneth Galbraith, requested the Indian government on several occasions to resolve the issue peacefully through mediation and consensus rather than armed conflict.[29][30]

On 24 November 1961, *Sabarmati*, a passenger boat passing between the Portuguese-held island of Anjidiv and the Indian port of Kochi, was fired upon by Portuguese ground troops, resulting in the death of a passenger and injuries to the chief engineer. The action was precipitated by Portuguese fears that the boat carried a military landing party intent on storming the island.[31] The incidents lent themselves to fostering widespread public support in India for military action in Goa.

Eventually, on 10 December, nine days prior to the "armed action (code named Operation Vijay)", Nehru stated to the press: "Continuance of Goa under Portuguese rule is an impossibility".[27] The American response was to warn India that if and when India's armed action in Goa was brought to the UN security council, it could expect no support from the US delegation.[32]

Annexation of Dadra and Nagar Haveli

This section does not cite any sources. Please help improve this section by adding citations to reliable sources. Unsourced material may be challenged and removed. *(December 2017)* (*Learn how and when to remove this template message*)

Main article: *Indian annexation of Dadra and Nagar Haveli*

The hostilities between India and Portugal started seven years before the annexation of Goa, when Dadra and Nagar Haveli were invaded and occupied by pro-Indian forces with the support of the Indian authorities.

Dadra and Nagar Haveli were two Portuguese landlocked exclaves of the Daman district, totally surrounded by Indian territory. The connection between the exclaves and the coastal territory of Daman had to be made by crossing about 20 kilometres (12 mi) of Indian territory. Dadra and Nagar Haveli did not have any Portuguese military garrison, but only police forces.

The Indian government started to develop isolation actions against Dadra and Nagar Haveli already in 1952, including the creation of impediments to the transit of persons and goods between the two landlocked enclaves and Daman. In July 1954, pro-Indian forces, including members of organisations like the United Front of Goans, the National Movement Liberation Organisation, the Rashtriya Swayamsevak Sangh and the Azad Gomantak Dal, with the support of Indian Police forces, began to launch assaults against Dadra and Nagar Haveli. On the night of 22 July, UFG forces stormed the small Dadra police station, killing Police Sergeant Aniceto do Rosário and Constable António Fernandes, who resisted the attack. On 28 July, RSS forces took Naroli police station.

Meanwhile, the Portuguese authorities asked the Indian Government for permission to cross the Indian territory with reinforcements to Dadra and Nagar Haveli, but no permission was given. Surrounded and prevented from receiving reinforcements by the Indian authorities, the Portuguese Administrator and police forces in Nagar Haveli eventually surrendered to the Indian police forces on 11 August 1954. Portugal appealed to the International Court of Justice, which, in a decision dated 12 April 1960,[33] stated that Portugal had sovereign rights over the territories of Dadra and Nagar Haveli but India had the right to deny passage to armed personnel of Portugal over Indian territories. Therefore, the Portuguese authorities could not legally pass through Indian territory.

Events preceding the hostilities

Indian military build-up

On receiving the go-ahead for military action and a mandate for the capture of all occupied territories for the Indian government, Lieutenant-General Chaudhari of India's Southern Army fielded the 17th Infantry Division and the 50th Parachute Brigade commanded by Major-General K. P. Candeth. The assault on the enclave of Daman was assigned to the 1st battalion of the Maratha Light Infantry while the operations in Diu were assigned to the 20th battalion of the Rajput Regiment and the 5th battalion of the Madras Regiment.[34]

Meanwhile, the Commander-in-Chief of India's Western Air Command, Air Vice Marshal Erlic Pinto, was appointed as the commander of all air resources assigned to the operations in Goa. Air resources for the assault on

Goa were concentrated in the bases at Pune and Sambra (Belgaum).[34] The mandate handed to Pinto by the Indian Air Command was listed out as follows:

1. The destruction of Goa's lone airfield in Dabolim, without causing damage to the terminal building and other airport facilities.
2. Destruction of the wireless station at Bambolim, Goa.
3. Denial of airfields at Daman and Diu, which were, however, not to be attacked without prior permission.
4. Support to advancing ground troops.

The Indian Navy deployed two warships—the INS *Rajput*, an 'R' Class destroyer, and INS *Kirpan*, a Blackwood class anti-submarine frigate—off the coast of Goa. The actual attack on Goa was delegated to four task groups: a Surface Action Group comprising five ships: *Mysore*, *Trishul*, *Betwa*, *Beas* and *Cauvery*; a Carrier Group of five ships: *Delhi*, *Kuthar*, *Kirpan*, *Khukri* and *Rajput* centred on the light aircraft carrier *Vikrant*; a Mine Sweeping Group consisting of mine sweepers including *Karwar*, *Kakinada*, *Cannonore* and *Bimilipatan*, and a Support Group which consisted of *Dharini*.[35]

Portuguese mandate

In March 1960, Portuguese Defence Minister General Júlio Botelho Moniz told Prime Minister Salazar that a sustained Portuguese campaign against decolonisation would create for the army "a suicide mission in which we could not succeed". His opinion was shared by Army Minister Colonel Afonso Magalhães de Almeida Fernandes, by the Army under secretary of State Lieutenant-Colonel Francisco da Costa Gomes and by other top officers.[36]

Ignoring this advice, Salazar sent a message to Governor General Manuel António Vassalo e Silva in Goa on 14 December, in which he ordered the Portuguese forces in Goa to fight to the last man: "Do not expect the possibility of truce or of Portuguese prisoners, as there will be no surrender rendered because I feel that our soldiers and sailors can be either victorious or dead."[37] Salazar asked Vassalo e Silva to hold out for at least eight days, within which time he hoped to gather international support against the Indian invasion. Vassalo e Silva disobeyed Salazar to avoid the unnecessary loss of human lives and surrendered the following day after the Indian invasion.[37]

Portuguese military preparations

Portuguese military preparations began in earnest in 1954, following the Indian economic blockade, the beginning of the anti-Portuguese attacks in Goa and the annexation of Dadra and Nagar Haveli. Three light infantry battalions (one each sent from Portugal, Angola and Mozambique) and support units were transported to Goa, reinforcing a locally raised battalion and increasing the Portuguese military presence there from almost nothing to 12,000 men.[15] Other sources state that, at the end of 1955, Portuguese forces in India represented a total of around 8,000 men (Europeans, Africans and Indians), including 7,000 in the land forces, 250 in the naval forces, 600 in the police and 250 in the Fiscal Guard, split between the districts of Goa, Daman and Diu.[38] Following the annexation of Dadra and Nagar Haveli, the Portuguese authorities markedly strengthened the garrison of Portuguese India, with units and personnel sent from the Metropole and from the Portuguese African provinces of Angola and Mozambique.

The Portuguese forces were organised as the Armed Forces of the State of India (FAEI, *Forças Armadas do Estado da Índia*), under a unified command headed by General Paulo Bénard Guedes, who combined the civil role of Governor-General with the military role of Commander-in-Chief. Guedes ended his commission in 1958, with General Vassalo e Silva being appointed to replace him in both the civil and military roles.[38]

The Portuguese government and military commands were, however, well aware that even with this effort to strengthen the garrison of Goa, the Portuguese forces would never be sufficient to face a conventional attack from the overwhelmingly stronger Indian Armed Forces. The Portuguese government hoped however to politically deter the Indian government from attempting a military aggression through the showing of a strong will to fight and to sacrifice to defend Goa.[38]

In 1960, during an inspection visit to Portuguese India and referring to a predictable start of guerrilla activities in Angola, the Under Secretary of State of the Army, Francisco da Costa Gomes, stated the necessity to reinforce the Portuguese military presence in that African territory, partly at the expense of the military presence in Goa, where the then existing 7,500 men were too many just to deal with anti-Portuguese actions, and too few to face an Indian invasion, which, if it were to occur, would have to be handled by other means. This led to the Portuguese forces in India suffering a sharp reduction to about 3,300 soldiers.[38]

Faced with this reduced force strength, the strategy employed to defend Goa against an Indian invasion was based on the *Plano Sentinela* (Sentinel Plan), which divided the territory into four defence sectors (North, Center, South and Mormugão), and the *Plano de Barragens* (Barrage Plan), which envisaged the demolition of all bridges to delay the invading army, as well as the mining of approach roads and beaches. Defence units were organised as four battlegroups (*agrupamentos*), with one assigned to each sector and tasked with slowing the progress of an invading force. Then-Captain Carlos Azaredo, who was stationed in Goa at the time of hostilities, described the Plano Sentinela in the Portuguese newspaper *Expresso* on 8 December 2001 as "a totally unrealistic and unachievable plan, which was quite incomplete. It was based on exchange of ground with time. But, for this purpose, portable communication equipment was necessary."[15] The plans to mine roads and beaches were also unviable because of a desperate shortage of mines.[39]

Navy

The naval component of the FAEI were the Naval Forces of the State of India (FNEI, *Forças Navais do Estado da Índia*), headed by the Naval Commander of Goa, Commodore Raúl Viegas Ventura. The only significant Portuguese Navy warship present in Goa at the time of invasion was the sloop NRP *Afonso de Albuquerque*.[40] It was armed with four 120 mm guns capable of two shots per minute, and four automatic rapid-firing guns. In addition to the sloop, the Portuguese Naval Forces had three light patrol boats (*lanchas de fiscalização*), each armed with a 20 mm Oerlikon gun, one based in each of Goa, Daman and Diu. There were also five merchant marine ships in Goa.[41] An attempt by Portugal to send naval warships to Goa to reinforce its marine defences was foiled when President Nasser of Egypt denied the ships access to the Suez Canal.[42][43][44]

Ground forces[edit]

Portuguese ground defences were organised as the Land Forces of the State of India (FTEI, *Forças Terrestres do Estado da Índia*), under the Portuguese Army's Independent Territorial Command of India, headed by Brigadier António José Martins Leitão. At the time of the invasion, they consisted of a total of 3,995 men, including 810 native (*Indo-Portugueses* – Indo-Portuguese) soldiers, many of whom had little military training and were utilised primarily for security and anti-extremist operations. These forces were divided amongst the three Portuguese enclaves in India.[38] The Portuguese Army units in Goa included four motorised reconnaissance squadrons, eight rifle companies (*caçadores*), two artillery batteries and an engineer detachment. In addition to the military forces, the Portuguese defences counted on the civil internal security forces of Portuguese India. These included the State of India Police (PEI, *Polícia do Estado da Índia*), a general police corps modelled after the Portuguese Public Security Police; the Fiscal Guard (*Guarda Fiscal*), responsible for Customs enforcement and border protection; and the Rural Guard (*Guarda Rural*), game wardens. In 1958, as an emergency measure, the Portuguese government gave provisional military status to the PEI and the Fiscal Guard, placing them under the command of the FAEI. The security forces were also divided amongst the three districts and were mostly made up of Indo-Portuguese policemen and guards. Different sources indicate between 900 and 1400 men as the total effective strength of these forces at the time of the invasion.[38]

Air defence

The Portuguese Air Force did not have any presence in Portuguese India, with the exception of a single officer with the role of air adviser in the office of the Commander-in-Chief.[38]

On 16 December, the Portuguese Air Force was placed on alert to transport ten tonnes of anti-tank grenades in two DC-6 aircraft from Montijo Air Base in Portugal to Goa to assist in its defence. When the Portuguese Air Force was unable to obtain stopover facilities at any air base along the way because most countries, including Pakistan, denied passage of Portuguese military aircraft, the mission was passed to the Portuguese international civilian airline TAP, which offered a Lockheed Constellation (registration CS-TLA) on charter. However, when permission to transport weapons through Karachi was denied by the Pakistani government, the Constellation landed in Goa at 18:00 on 17 December with a consignment of half a dozen bags of sausages as food supplies instead of the intended grenades. In addition it transported a contingent of female paratroopers to assist in the evacuation of Portuguese civilians.[45]

The Portuguese air presence in Goa at the time of hostilities was thus limited to the presence of two civilian transport aircraft, the Lockheed Constellation belonging to TAP and a Douglas DC-4 Skymaster belonging to the Goan airline Portuguese India Airlines. The Indians claimed that the Portuguese had a squadron of F-86 Sabres stationed at Dabolim Airport—which later turned out to be false intelligence. Air defence was limited to a few obsolete anti-aircraft guns manned by two artillery units who had been smuggled into Goa disguised as football teams.[31]

Portuguese civilian evacuation

The military buildup created panic amongst Europeans in Goa, who were desperate to evacuate their families before the commencement of hostilities. On 9 December, the vessel *India* arrived at Goa's Mormugão port en route to Lisbon from Timor. Despite orders from the Portuguese government in Lisbon not to allow anyone to embark on this vessel, Governor General Manuel Vassalo e Silva allowed 700 Portuguese civilians of European origin to board the ship and flee Goa. The ship had capacity for only 380 passengers, and was filled to its limits, with evacuees occupying even the toilets.[31] On arranging this evacuation of women and children, Vassalo e Silva remarked to the press, "If necessary, we will die here." Evacuation of European civilians continued by air even after the commencement of Indian air strikes.[46]

Indian reconnaissance operations

Indian reconnaissance operations had commenced on 1 December, when two Leopard class frigates, the INS *Betwa* and the INS *Beas*, undertook linear patrolling of the Goa coast at a distance of 8 miles (13 km). By 8 December, the Indian Air Force had commenced baiting missions and fly-bys to lure out Portuguese air defences and fighters.[*citation needed*]

On 17 December, a tactical reconnaissance flight conducted by Squadron Leader I. S. Loughran in a Vampire NF54 Night Fighter over Dabolim Airport in Goa was met with five rounds fired from a ground anti-aircraft gun. The aircraft took evasive action by drastically dropping altitude and escaping out to sea. The anti-aircraft gun was later recovered near the ATC building with a round jammed in its breech.[47]

The Indian light aircraft carrier INS *Vikrant* was deployed 75 miles (121 km) off the coast of Goa to head a possible amphibious operation on Goa, as well as to deter any foreign military intervention.

Commencement of hostilities

Military actions in Goa

Ground attack on Goa: North and North East sectors

This section **needs additional citations for** verification. Please help improve this article by adding citations to reliable sources. Unsourced material may be challenged and removed.
Find sources: "Annexation of Goa" – news · newspapers · books · scholar · JSTOR *(May 2018) (Learn how and when to*

remove this template message)

On 11 December 1961, 17th Infantry Division and attached troops of the Indian Army were ordered to advance into Goa to capture Panaji and Mormugão. The main thrust on Panaji was to be made by the 50th Para Brigade Group, led by Brigadier Sagat Singh from the north. Another thrust was to be carried out by 63rd Indian Infantry Brigade from the east. A deceptive thrust, in company strength, was to be made from the south along the Majali-Canacona-Margao axis.[48]

Although the 50th Para Brigade was charged with merely assisting the main thrust conducted by the 17th Infantry, its units moved rapidly across minefields, roadblocks and four riverine obstacles to be the first to reach Panaji.[49]

Hostilities at Goa began at 09:45 on 17 December 1961, when a unit of Indian troops attacked and occupied the town of Maulinguém in the north east, killing two Portuguese soldiers. The Portuguese 2nd EREC (*esquadrão de reconhecimento*—reconnaissance squadron), stationed near Maulinguém, asked for permission to engage the Indians, but permission was refused at about 13:45.[50] During the afternoon of the 17th, the Portuguese command issued instructions that all orders to defending troops would be issued directly by headquarters, bypassing the local command outposts. This led to confusion in the chain of command.[50] At 02:00 on 18 December, the 2nd EREC was sent to the town of Doromagogo to support the withdrawal of police forces present in the area, and were attacked by Indian Army units on their return journey.[50]

At 04:00, the Indian assault commenced with artillery bombardment on Portuguese positions south of Maulinguém, launched on the basis of the false intelligence that the Portuguese had stationed heavy battle tanks in the area. By 04:30, Bicholim was under fire. At 04:40, the Portuguese forces destroyed the bridge at Bicholim and followed this with the destruction of the bridges at Chapora in Colvale and at Assonora at 05:00.[50]

On the morning of 18 December, the 50th Para Brigade of the Indian Army moved into Goa in three columns.

1. The eastern column comprised the 2nd Para Maratha advanced towards the town of Ponda in central Goa via Usgão.
2. The central column consisting of the 1st Para Punjab advanced towards Panaji via the village of Banastari.
3. The western column—the main thrust of the attack—comprised the 2nd Sikh Light Infantry as well as an armoured division which crossed the border at 06:30 and advanced on Tivim.[48]

At 05:30, Portuguese troops left their barracks at Ponda in central Goa and marched towards the town of Usgão, in the direction of the advancing eastern column of the Indian 2nd Para Maratha, which was under the command of Major Dalip Singh Jind and included tanks of the Indian 7th Cavalry. At 09:00, these Portuguese troops reported that Indian troops had already covered half the distance to the town of Ponda.[50]

Indian troops being greeted by supporters as they march through the streets of Panaji shortly after the Portuguese retreat

By 10:00, Portuguese forces of the 1st EREC, faced with the advancing 2nd Sikh Light Infantry, began a south-bound withdrawal to the town of Mapuca where, by 12:00, they came under the risk of being surrounded by Indian forces. At 12:30, the 1st EREC began a retreat, making their way through the Indian forces, with their armoured cars firing ahead to cover the withdrawal of the personnel carrier vehicles. This unit relocated by ferry further south to the capital city of Panaji.[50] At 13:30, just after the retreat of the 2nd EREC, the Portuguese destroyed the bridge at Banastarim, cutting off all road links to Panaji.

By 17:45, the forces of the 1st EREC and the 9th *Caçadores* Company of the Portuguese Battlegroup North had completed their ferry crossing of the Mandovi River to Panaji, just minutes ahead of the arrival of the Indian armoured forces.[50] The Indian tanks had reached Betim, just across the Mandovi River from Panaji, without encountering any opposition. The 2nd Sikh Light Infantry joined it by 21:00, crossing over mines and demolished bridges en route. In the absence of orders, the unit stayed at Betim for the night.

At 20:00, a Goan by the name of Gregório Magno Antão crossed the Mandovi River from Panaji and delivered a ceasefire offer letter from Major Acácio Tenreiro of the Portuguese Army to Major Shivdev Singh Sidhu, the commanding officer of the Indian 7th Cavalry camped there. The letter read: "The Military Commander of the City of Goa states that he wishes to parley with the commander of the army of the Indian Union with respect to the surrender. Under these conditions, the Portuguese troops must immediately cease fire and the Indian troops do likewise in order to prevent the slaughter of the population and the destruction of the city." [51]

The same night Major Shivdev Singh Sidhu with a force of the 7th Cavalry decided to take Fort Aguada and obtain its surrender, after receiving information that a number of supporters of the Indian Republic were held prisoners there. However, the Portuguese defenders of the fort had not yet received orders to surrender and responded by opening fire on the Indian forces, Major Sidhu and Captain Vinod Sehgal being killed in the firefight.[48]

The order for Indian forces to cross the Mandovi River was received on the morning of 19 December, upon which two rifle companies of the 2nd Sikh Light Infantry advanced on Panaji at 07:30 and secured the town without facing any resistance. On orders from Brigadier Sagat Singh, the troops entering Panaji removed their steel helmets and donned the Parachute Regiment's maroon berets. Fort Aguada was also captured on that day, when the Indian 7th Cavalry attacked with assistance from the armoured division stationed at Betim and freed its political prisoners.

Advance from the east[edit]

This section **does not** cite any sources. Please help improve this section by adding citations to reliable sources. Unsourced material may be challenged and removed. *(May 2018)* (*Learn how and when to remove this template message*)

Meanwhile, in the east, the 63rd Indian Infantry Brigade advanced in two columns. The right column, consisting of the 2nd Bihar Battalion, and the left column, consisting of the 3rd Sikh Battalion, linked up at the border town of Mollem and then advanced by separate routes on Ponda. By nightfall, the 2nd Bihar had reached the town of Candeapur, while the 3rd Sikh had reached Darbondara. Although neither column had encountered any resistance, their further progress was hampered because all bridges spanning the river had been destroyed.

The rear battalion was the 4th Sikh Infantry, which reached Candeapar in the early hours of 19 December, and not to be bogged down by the destruction of the Borim bridge, went across the Zuari river in their military tankers and then waded through chest-high water across a small stream to reach a dock known as Embarcadouro de Tembim in the village of Raia, from where a road connects to Margão, the administrative centre of southern Goa. Their rear battalion took some rest in a cattle shed and on the grounds and the balcony of an adjacent house before proceeding to Margão by 12:00. From here, the column advanced towards the harbour of Mormugão. En route they encountered fierce resistance from a 500-strong Portuguese unit at the village of Verna, where they were joined by the 2nd Bihar. The Portuguese unit surrendered at 15:30 after fierce fighting, and the 4th Sikh then proceeded to Mormugão and Dabolim Airport, where the main body of the Portuguese Army awaited the Indians.

The 4th Rajput company staged a decoy attack south of Margão in order to mislead the Portuguese. This column overcame minefields, roadblocks and demolished bridges, and eventually went on to help secure the town of Margão.

Air raids over Goa

A Canberra PR.9 taking off. The Indian Air Force used 20 small and lightweight Canberra bombers.

The first Indian raid was led by Wing Commander N.B. Menon on 18 December on the Dabolim Airport using 12 English Electric Canberra aircraft. 63,000 pounds of explosives were dropped within minutes, completely destroying the runway. In line with the mandate given by the Air Command, structures and facilities at the airfield were left undamaged.[34]

The second Indian raid was conducted on the same target by eight Canberras led by Wing Commander Surinder Singh, again leaving the airport's terminal and other buildings untouched. Two civilian transport aircraft—a Lockheed Constellation belonging to the Portuguese airline TAP and a Douglas DC-4 belonging to the Goan airline TAIP—were parked on the apron. On the night of 18 December, the Portuguese used both aircraft to evacuate the families of some government and military officials after airport workers had hastily recovered part of the heavily damaged runway that evening. The first aircraft to leave was the TAP Constellation, commanded by Manuel Correia Reis, which took off using only 700 metres; debris from the runway damaged the fuselage, causing 25 holes and a flat tire. To make the 'short take-off' possible, the pilots had jettisoned all the extra seats and other unwanted equipment.[52] The TAIP DC-4 then also took off, piloted by TAIP Director Major Solano de Almeida. The two aircraft successfully used the cover of night and very low altitudes to break through Indian aerial patrols and escape to Karachi, Pakistan.[53]

A third Indian raid was carried out by six Hawker Hunters, successfully targeting the wireless station at Bambolim with rockets and gun cannons.

The mandate to support ground troops was served by the de Havilland Vampires of No. 45 squadron, which patrolled the sector but did not receive any requests into action. In an incident of friendly fire, two Vampires fired rockets into the positions of the 2nd Sikh Light Infantry, injuring two soldiers, while elsewhere, Indian ground troops mistakenly opened fire on an IAF T-6 Texan, causing minimal damage.

In later years, commentators have maintained that India's intense air strikes against the airfields were uncalled-for, since none of the targeted airports had any military capabilities and they did not cater to any military aircraft. As such, the airfields were defenceless civilian targets.[53] The Indian navy continues to control the Dabolim Airport, although it is also once more used as a civilian airport.

Storming of Anjidiv Island[edit]

This section **does** not cite any sources. Please help improve this section by adding citations to reliable sources. Unsourced material may be challenged and removed. *(May 2018) (Learn how and when to remove this template message)*

Anjidiv was a small 1.5 km² island of Portuguese India, then almost uninhabited, belonging to the District of Goa, although off the coast of the Indian state of Karnataka. On the island stood the ancient Anjidiv Fort, defended by a platoon of Goan soldiers of the Portuguese Army.

The Indian Naval Command assigned the task of securing Anjidiv to the cruiser INS *Mysore* and the frigate INS *Trishul*. Under covering artillery fire from the ships, Indian marines under the command of Lieutenant Arun Auditto stormed the island at 14:25 on 18 December and engaged the Portuguese garrison. The assault was repulsed by the Portuguese defenders, with seven Indian marines killed and 19 wounded. Among the Indian casualties were two officers.

The Portuguese defences were eventually overrun after fierce shelling from the Indian ships offshore. The island was secured by the Indians at 14:00 on the next day, all the Portuguese defenders being captured with the exception of two corporals and one private. Hidden in the rocks, one corporal surrendered on 19 December. The other was captured in the afternoon of 20 December, but not before launching hand grenades that injured several Indian marines. The last of the three, Goan private Manuel Caetano, became the last Portuguese soldier in India to be captured, on 22 December, after he had reached the Indian shore by swimming.

Naval battle at Mormugão harbour[edit]

The NRP *Afonso de Albuquerque*

On the morning of 18 December, the Portuguese sloop NRP *Afonso de Albuquerque* was anchored off Mormugão Harbour. Besides engaging Indian naval units, the ship was also tasked with providing a coastal artillery battery to defend the harbour and adjoining beaches, and providing vital radio communications with Lisbon after on-shore radio facilities had been destroyed in Indian airstrikes.

At 09:00, three Indian frigates led by the INS *Betwa* took up position off the harbour, awaiting orders to attack the *Afonso* and secure sea access to the port. At 11:00, Indian planes bombed Mormugão harbour.[3] At 12:00, upon receiving clearance, the INS *Betwa* and the INS *Beas* entered the harbour and fired on the *Afonso* with their 4.5-inch guns while transmitting requests to surrender in morse code between shots. In response, the *Afonso* lifted anchor, headed out towards the enemy and returned fire with its 120 mm guns.

The *Afonso* was outnumbered by the Indians, and was at a severe disadvantage since it was in a confined position that restricted its manoeuvring, and because its four 120 mm guns could fire only two rounds a minute, as compared to the 16 rounds per minute of the guns aboard the Indian frigates. A few minutes into the exchange of fire, at 12:15, the *Afonso* took a direct hit in its control tower, injuring its weapons officer. At 12:25, an anti-personnel shrapnel bomb fired from an Indian vessel exploded directly over the ship, killing its radio officer and severely injuring its commander, Captain António da Cunha Aragão, after which First Officer Pinto da Cruz took command of the vessel. The ship's propulsion system was also badly damaged in this attack.

At 12:35, the *Afonso* swerved 180 degrees and was run aground against Bambolim beach. At that time, against the commander's orders, a white flag was hoisted under instructions from the sergeant in charge of signals, but the flag coiled itself around the mast and as a result was not spotted by the Indians, who continued their barrage. The flag was immediately lowered.

Eventually at 12:50, after the *Afonso* had fired nearly 400 rounds at the Indians, hitting two of the Indian vessels, and had taken severe damage, the order was given to start abandoning ship. Under heavy fire directed at both the ship and the coast, non-essential crew including weapons staff left the ship and went ashore. They were followed at 13:10 by the rest of the crew, who, along with their injured commander, set fire to the ship and disembarked directly onto the beach. Following this, the commander was transferred by car to the hospital at Panaji. The NRP *Afonso de Albuquerque* lost 5 dead and 13 wounded in the battle.[3]

The sloop's crew formally surrendered with the remaining Portuguese forces on 19 December 1961 at 20:30.[15] As a gesture of goodwill, the commanders of the INS *Betwa* and the INS *Beas* later visited Captain Aragão as he lay recuperating in bed in Panaji.

The *Afonso*—having been renamed *Saravastri* by the Indian Navy—lay grounded at the beach near Dona Paula until 1962, when it was towed to Bombay and sold for scrap. Parts of the ship were recovered and are on display at the Naval Museum in Bombay.[3]

The Portuguese patrol boat NRP *Sirius*, under the command of Lieutenant Marques Silva, was also present at Goa. After observing *Afonso* running aground and not having communications from the Goa Naval Command, Lieutenant Marques Silva decided to scuttle the *Sirius*. This was done by damaging the propellers and making the boat hit the rocks. The eight men of the *Sirius*'s crew avoided being captured by the Indian forces and boarded a Greek freighter on which they reached Pakistan.

Military actions in Daman

Ground attack on Daman

Daman, approximately 72 km² in area, is at the south end of Gujarat bordering Maharashtra, approximately 193 km north of Bombay. The countryside is broken and interspersed with marsh, salt pans, streams, paddy fields, coconut and palm groves. The river Daman Ganga splits the capital city of Daman (Damão in Portuguese) into halves—Nani Daman (*Damão Pequeno*) and Moti Daman (*Damão Grande*). The strategically important features were Daman Fort (fortress of São Jerónimo) and the air control tower of Daman Airport.[54]

The Portuguese garrison in Daman was headed by Major António José da Costa Pinto (combining the roles of District Governor and military commander), with 360 soldiers of the Portuguese Army, 200 policemen and about 30 customs officials under him. The army forces consisted of two companies of *caçadores* (light infantry) and an artillery battery, organised as the battlegroup "Constantino de Bragança". The artillery battery was armed with 87.6 mm guns, but these had insufficient and old ammunition. The Portuguese also placed a 20 mm anti-aircraft gun ten days before the invasion to protect the artillery. Daman had been secured with small minefields and defensive shelters had been built.[41]

The advance on the enclave of Daman was conducted by the 1st Maratha Light Infantry Battalion under the command of Lieutenant-Colonel S.J.S. Bhonsle[54] in a pre-dawn operation on 18 December.[48] The plan was to capture Daman piecemeal in four phases, starting with the area of the airfield, then progressively the open countryside, Damão Pequeno and finally Damão Grande including the fort.[54]

The advance commenced at 04:00 when one battalion and three companies of Indian soldiers progressed through the central area of the northern territory, aiming to seize the airfield.[41] However, the surprise was lost when the Indian A Company tried to capture the control tower and suffered three casualties. The Portuguese lost one soldier dead and six taken captive. The Indian D Company captured a position named "Point 365" just before the next morning. At the crack of dawn, two sorties by Indian Air Force Mystère fighters struck Portuguese mortar positions and guns inside Moti Daman Fort.[54]

At 04:30, the Indian artillery began to bombard Damão Grande. The artillery attack and transportation difficulties isolated the Portuguese command post there from the forces in Damão Pequeno. At 07:30, a Portuguese unit at the fortress of São Jerónimo fired mortars on Indian forces attempting to capture the airstrip.[41]

At 11:30, Portuguese forces resisting an Indian advance on the eastern border at Varacunda ran out of ammunition and withdrew westwards to Catra. At 12:00, to delay the Indian advance following the withdrawal from Varacunda, the Portuguese artillery battery on the banks of the Rio Sandalcalo was ordered to open fire. The commander of the battery, Captain Felgueiras de Sousa, instead dismantled the guns and surrendered to the Indians.[41] By 12:00, the airfield was assaulted by the Indian A and C companies simultaneously. In the ensuing exchange of fire the A Company lost one more soldier and seven were wounded.[54]

By 13:00, the remaining Portuguese forces on the east border at Calicachigão exhausted their ammunition and retreated towards the coast. By 17:00, in the absence of resistance, the Indians had managed to occupy most of the territory, except the airfield and Damão Pequeno, where the Portuguese were making their last stand. By this time, the Indian Air Force had conducted six air attacks, severely demoralising the Portuguese forces. At 20:00, after a meeting between the Portuguese commanders, a delegation was dispatched to the Indian lines to open negotiations, but was fired on, and was forced to withdraw. A similar attempt by the artillery to surrender at 08:00 next day was also fired on.[41]

The Indians assaulted the airfield the next morning, upon which the Portuguese surrendered at 11:00 without a fight.[48] Garrison commander Major Costa Pinto, although wounded, was stretchered to the airfield, as the Indians were only willing to accept a surrender from him.[41] Approximately 600 Portuguese soldiers and policemen (including 24 officers[54]) were taken prisoner. The Indians suffered 4 dead and 14 wounded,[54] while the Portuguese suffered 10 dead and two wounded.[48] The 1st Light Maratha Infantry was decorated for the battle with one VSM for the commanding officer, two Sena Medals and five Mentioned in Dispatches.[54]

Daman air raids

In the Daman sector, Indian Mystères flew 14 sorties, continuously harassing Portuguese artillery positions.

Naval action at Daman[edit]

This section **does not** cite any sources. Please help improve this section by adding citations to reliable sources. Unsourced material may be challenged and removed. *(May 2018) (Learn how and when to remove this template message)*

Like the *Vega* in Diu, the patrol boat NRP *Antares*—based at Daman under the command of 2nd Lieutenant Abreu Brito—was ordered to sail out and fight the imminent Indian invasion. The boat stayed in position from 07:00 on 18 December and remained a mute witness to repeated air strikes followed by ground invasion until 19:20, when it lost all communications with land.

With all information pointing to total occupation of all Portuguese enclaves in India, Lieutenant Brito decided to save his crew and vessel by escaping; the *Vega* traversed 530 miles (850 km), escaping detection by Indian forces, and arrived at Karachi at 20:00 on 20 December.

Military actions in Diu

Ground attack on Diu

Diu is a 13.8 km by 4.6 km island (area about 40 km²) at the south tip of Gujarat. The island is separated from the mainland by a narrow channel running through a swamp. The channel could only be used by fishing boats and small craft. No bridges crossed the channels at the time of hostilities. The Portuguese garrison in Diu was headed by Major Fernando de Almeida e Vasconcelos (district governor and military commander), with around 400 soldiers and police officers, organised as the battlegroup "António da Silveira".[55]

Diu was attacked on 18 December from the north west along Kob Forte by two companies of the 20th Rajput Battalion—with the capture of the Diu Airfield being the primary objective—and from the northeast along Gogal and Amdepur by the Rajput B Company and the 4th Madras Battalion.[48]

These Indian Army units ignored requests from Wing Commander M.P.O. "Micky" Blake, planning-in-charge of the Indian Air Force operations in Diu, to attack only on first light when close air support would be available.[55] The Portuguese defences repulsed the attack backed by 87.6mm artillery and mortars,[41] inflicting heavy losses on the Indians.[55] The first attack was made by the 4th Madras on a police border post at 01:30 on 18 December at Gogol and was repulsed by 13 Portuguese police officers.[41] Another attempt by the 4th Madras at 02:00 was again repulsed, this time backed with Portuguese 87.5mm artillery and mortar which suffered due to poor quality of munitions. By 04:00, ten of the original 13 Portuguese defenders at Gogol had been wounded and were evacuated to a hospital. At 05:30, the Portuguese artillery launched a fresh attack on the 4th Madras assaulting Gogol and forced their retreat.[41]

Meanwhile, at 03:00, two companies of the 20th Rajput attempted to cross a muddy swamp[41] separating them from the Portuguese forces at Passo Covo under cover of dark on rafts made of bamboo cots tied to oil barrels.[55] The attempt was to establish a bridgehead and capture the airfield.[48]

This attack was repulsed with fairly heavy losses by a well entrenched unit of Portuguese soldiers armed with small automatic weapons and Sten guns[55] as well as light and medium machine guns. According to Indian sources this unit included between 125 and 130 soldiers,[48] but according to Portuguese sources this post was defended by only eight soldiers.[41]

As the Rajputs reached the middle of the creek, the Portuguese on Diu opened fire with two medium and two light machine-guns, capsizing some of the rafts. Major Mal Singh of the Indian Army along with five men pressed on his advance and crossed the creek. On reaching the far bank, he and his men assaulted the light machine gun trenches at Fort-De-Cova and silenced them. The Portuguese medium machine gun fire from another position wounded the officer and two of his men. However, with the efforts of company Havildar Major Mohan Singh and two other men, the three wounded were evacuated back across the creek to safety. As dawn approached, the Portuguese increased the intensity of fire and the battalion's water crossing equipment suffered extensive damage. As a result, the Indian battalion was ordered to fall back to Kob village by first light.[54]

Another assault at 05:00 was similarly repulsed by the Portuguese defenders. At 06:30, Portuguese forces retrieved rafts abandoned by the 20th Rajput, recovered ammunition left behind and rescued a wounded Indian soldier, who was given treatment.[41]

At 07:00, with the onset of dawn, Indian air strikes began, forcing the Portuguese to retreat from Passo Covo to the town of Malala. By 09:00 the Portuguese unit at Gogol also retreated,[41] allowing the Rajput B Company (who replaced the 4th Madras) to advance under heavy artillery fire and occupy the town.[48] By 10:15, the Indian cruiser INS Delhi, anchored off Diu, began to bombard targets on the shore.[41] At 12:45, Indian jets fired a rocket at a mortar at Diu Fortress causing a fire near a munitions dump, forcing the Portuguese to order the evacuation of the fortress—a task completed by 14:15 under heavy bombardment from the Indians.[41]

At 18:00, the Portuguese commanders agreed in a meeting that, in view of repeated air strikes and the inability to establish contact with headquarters in Goa or Lisbon, there was no way to pursue an effective defence and decided to surrender to the Indians.[41] On 19 December, by 12:00, the Portuguese formally surrendered. The Indians took 403 prisoners, which included the Governor of the island along with 18 officers and 43 sergeants.[54]

In surrendering to the Indians, the Diu Governor stated that he could have kept the Army out for a few weeks but he had no answer to the Air Force. The Indian Air Force was also present at the ceremony and was represented by Gp Capt Godkhindi, Wing Cmdr Micky Blake and Sqn Ldr Nobby Clarke.[55] 7 Portuguese soldiers were killed in the battle.[55]

Major Mal Singh and Sepoy Hakam Singh of the Indian army were awarded Ashok Chakra (Class III).[54]

On 19 December, the 4th Madras C Company landed on the island of Panikot off Diu, where a group of 13 Portuguese soldiers surrendered to them there.[48]

The Diu air raids

A MD450 Ouragan on display at the "Royal Museum of Armed Forces and Military History" (Brussels-Belgium). Similar aircraft in service with the Indian Air Force, locally known as Toofani, formed the backbone of the air strikes on Diu.

The Indian air operations in the Diu Sector were entrusted to the Armaments Training Wing led by Wg Cdr Micky Blake. The first air attacks were made at dawn on 18 December and were aimed at destroying Diu's fortifications facing the mainland. Throughout the rest of the day, the Air Force had at least two aircraft in the air at any time, giving close support to advancing Indian infantry. During the morning, the air force attacked and destroyed Diu Airfield's ATC as well as parts of Diu Fort. On orders from Tactical Air Command located at Pune, a sortie of two Toofanis attacked and destroyed the airfield runway with 4 1000 lb Mk 9 bombs. A second sortie aimed at the runway and piloted by Wg Cdr Blake himself was aborted when Blake detected what he reported as people waving white flags. In subsequent sorties, the Indian Air Force attacked and destroyed the Portuguese ammunition dump as well a patrol boat that attempted to escape from Diu.

In the absence of any Portuguese air presence, Portuguese ground-based anti-aircraft units attempted to offer resistance to the Indian raids, but were overwhelmed and quickly silenced, leaving complete air superiority to the

Indians. Continued air attacks forced the Portuguese governor of Diu to surrender.

Naval action at Diu

The Indian cruiser INS *Delhi* was anchored off the coast of Diu and fired a barrage from its 6-inch guns at the Portuguese occupied Diu Fortress. The Commanding Officer of the Indian Air Force operating in the area reported that some of the shells fired from the *New Delhi* were bouncing off the beach and exploding on the Indian mainland. However, no casualties were reported from this.[56]

At 04:00 on 18 December, the Portuguese patrol boat NRP *Vega* encountered the *New Delhi* around 12 miles (19 km) off the coast of Diu, and was attacked with heavy machine gun fire. Staying out of range, the boat had no casualties and minimal damage, the boat withdrew to the port at Diu.

At 07:00, news was received that the Indian invasion had commenced, and the commander of the *Vega*, 2nd Lt Oliveira e Carmo was ordered to sail out and fight until the last round of ammunition. At 07:30 the crew of the *Vega* spotted two Indian aircraft on patrol missions and opened fire on them with the ship's 20mm Oerlikon gun. In retaliation the Indian aircraft attacked the *Vega* twice, killing the captain and the gunner and forcing the rest of the crew to abandon the boat and swim ashore, where they were taken prisoners of war.

UN attempts at ceasefire

On 18 December, a Portuguese request was made to the UN Security Council for a debate on the conflict in Goa. The request was approved when the bare minimum of seven members supported the request (the US, UK, France, Turkey, Chile, Ecuador, and Nationalist China), two opposed (the Soviet Union and Ceylon), and two abstained (the United Arab Republic and Liberia).[57]

Opening the debate, Portugal's delegate, Vasco Vieira Garin, said that Portugal had consistently shown her peaceful intentions by refraining from any counter-action to India's numerous "provocations" on the Goan border. Garin also stated that Portuguese forces, though "vastly outnumbered by the invading forces," were putting up "stiff resistance" and "fighting a delaying action and destroying communications in order to halt the advance of the enemy." In response, India's delegate, Jha said that the "elimination of the last vestiges of colonialism in India" was an "article of faith" for the Indian people, "Security Council or no Security Council." He went on to describe Goa, Daman, and Diu as "an inalienable part of India unlawfully occupied by Portugal."[57]

In the ensuing debate, the US delegate, Adlai Stevenson, strongly criticised India's use of force to resolve her dispute with Portugal, stressing that such resort to violent means was against the charter of the UN. He stated that condoning such acts of armed forces would encourage other nations to resort to similar solutions to their own disputes, and would lead to the death of the United Nations. In response, the Soviet delegate, Valerian Zorin, argued that the Goan question was wholly within India's domestic jurisdiction and could not be considered by the Security Council. He also drew attention to Portugal's disregard for UN resolutions calling for the granting of independence to colonial countries and peoples.[57]

Following the debate, the delegates of Liberia, Ceylon and the U.A.R. presented a resolution which: (1) stated that "the enclaves claimed by Portugal in India constitute a threat to international peace and security and stand in the way of the unity of the Republic of India; (2) asked the security Council to reject the Portuguese charge of aggression against India; and (3) called upon Portugal "to terminate hostile action and co-operate with India in the liquidation of her colonial possessions in India." This resolution was supported only by the Soviet Union, the other seven members opposing.[57]

After the defeat of the Afro-Asian resolution, a resolution was presented by France, Turkey, the United Kingdom and the United States which: (1) Called for the immediate cessation of hostilities; (2) Called upon India to withdraw her forces immediately to "the positions prevailing before 17 Dec 1961." (3) Urged India and Portugal "to work out a permanent solution of their differences by peaceful means in accordance with the principles embodied in the Charter"; and (4) Requested the U.N. Secretary-General "to provide such assistance as may be appropriate."[57]

This resolution received seven votes in favour (the four sponsors and Chile, Ecuador, and Nationalist China) and four against (the Soviet Union, Ceylon, Liberia, and the United Arab Republic). It was thus defeated by the Soviet veto. In a statement after the vote, Mr. Stevenson said that the "fateful" Goa debate could have been be "the first act of a drama" which could have ended in the death of the United Nations.[57]

Portuguese surrender

Lt Col Sucha Singh, CO 1 PARA, of India's Maroon Beret Parachute regiment accepts the surrender of Portuguese forces at a military camp in Bambolim.

By the evening of 18 December, most of Goa had been overrun by advancing Indian forces, and a large party of more than two thousand Portuguese soldiers had taken position at the military base at Alparqueiros at the entrance to the port town of Vasco da Gama. Per the Portuguese strategy code named *Plano Sentinela* the defending forces were to make their last stand at the harbour, holding out against the Indians until Portuguese naval reinforcements could arrive. Orders delivered from the Portuguese President called for a scorched earth policy—that Goa was to be destroyed before it was given up to the Indians.[58] Canadian political scientist Antonio Rangel Bandeira has argued that the sacrifice of Goa was an elaborate public relations stunt calculated to rally support for Portugal's wars in Africa.[36][*page needed*]

Despite his orders from Lisbon, Governor General Manuel António Vassalo e Silva took stock of the numerical superiority of the Indian troops, as well as the food and ammunition supplies available to his forces and took the decision to surrender. He later described his orders to destroy Goa as "*um sacrifício inútil*" (a useless sacrifice).[*citation needed*]

The Indian Chief of Army Staff, General Pran Thapar (far right) with deposed Governor General of Portuguese India Manuel António Vassalo e Silva (seated centre) at a POW facility in Vasco Da Gama, Goa

In a communication to all Portuguese forces under his command, he stated, "Having considered the defence of the Peninsula of Mormugão... from aerial, naval and ground fire of the enemy and ... having considered the difference between the forces and the resources... the situation does not allow myself to proceed with the fight without great sacrifice of the lives of the inhabitants of Vasco da Gama, I have decided with ... my patriotism well present, to get in touch with the enemy ... I order all my forces to cease-fire."[59]

The official Portuguese surrender was conducted in a formal ceremony held at 2030 hours on 19 December when Governor General Manuel António Vassalo e Silva signed the instrument of surrender bringing to an end 451 years of Portuguese Rule in Goa. In all, 4668 personnel were taken prisoner by the Indians—a figure which included military and civilian personnel, Portuguese, Africans and Goan.[15]

Upon the surrender of the Portuguese governor general, Goa, Daman and Diu was declared a federally administered Union Territory placed directly under the President of India, and Major-General K. P. Candeth was appointed as its military governor. The war had lasted two days, and had cost 22 Indian and 30 Portuguese lives.

Those Indian forces who served within the disputed territories for 48 hours, or flew at least one operational sortie during the conflict, received a General Service Medal 1947 with the *Goa 1961* bar.[60]

Portuguese actions post-hostilities

When they received news of the fall of Goa, the Portuguese government formally severed all diplomatic links with India and refused to recognise the incorporation of the seized territories into the Indian Republic. An offer of Portuguese citizenship was instead made to all Goan natives who wished to emigrate to Portugal rather than remain under Indian rule. This was amended in 2006 to include only those who had been born before 19 December 1961. Later, in a show of defiance, Prime Minister Salazar's government offered a reward of US$10,000 for the capture of Brigadier Sagat Singh, the commander of the maroon berets of India's parachute regiment who were the first troops to enter Panaji, Goa's capital.[61]

Lisbon went virtually into mourning, and Christmas celebrations were extremely muted. Cinemas and theatres shut down as tens of thousands of Portuguese marched in a silent parade from Lisbon's city hall to the cathedral, escorting the relics of St. Francis Xavier.[62]

Salazar, while addressing the Portuguese National Assembly on 3 January 1962, invoked the principle of national sovereignty, as defined in the legal framework of the Constitution of the Estado Novo. "We can not negotiate, not without denying and betraying our own, the cession of national territory and the transfer of populations that inhabit them to foreign sovereigns," said Salazar.[63] He went on to state that the UN's failure to halt aggression against Portugal, showed that effective power in the U.N. had passed to the Communist and Afro-Asian countries. Dr. Salazar also accused Britain of delaying for a week her reply to Portugal's request to be allowed the use of certain airfields. "Had it not been for this delay," he said, "we should certainly have found alternative routes and we could have rushed to India reinforcements in men and material for a sustained defence of the territory."[57]

Hinting that Portugal would yet be vindicated, Salazar went on to state that "difficulties will arise for both sides when the programme of the Indianization of Goa begins to clash with its inherent culture... It is therefore to be expected that many Goans will wish to escape to Portugal from the inevitable consequences of the invasion."[57]

In the months after the conflict, the Portuguese Government used broadcasts on Emissora Nacional, the Portuguese national radio station, to urge Goans to resist and oppose the Indian administration. An effort was made to create clandestine resistance movements in Goa, and within Goan diaspora communities across the world to use general resistance and armed rebellion to weaken the Indian presence in Goa. The campaign had the full support of the Portuguese government with the ministries of defence, foreign affairs, army, navy and finance involved. A plan was chalked out called the 'Plano Gralha' covering Goa, Daman and Diu, which called for paralysing port operations at Mormugao and Bombay by planting bombs in some of the ships anchored at the ports.[64][65]

On 20 June 1964, Casimiro Monteiro, a Portuguese PIDE agent of Goan descent, along with Ismail Dias, a Goan settled in Portugal, executed a series of bombings in Goa.[66]

Relations between India and Portugal thawed only in 1974, when, following an anti-colonial military coup d'état and the fall of the authoritarian rule in Lisbon, Goa was finally recognised as part of India, and steps were taken to re-establish diplomatic relations with India. On 31 December 1974, a treaty was signed between India and Portugal with the Portuguese recognising full sovereignty of India over Goa, Daman, Diu, Dadra and Nagar Haveli.[67] In 1992, Portuguese President Mário Soares became the first Portuguese head of state to visit Goa after its annexation by India, following Indian President R. Venkataraman's visit to Portugal in 1990.[68]

Internment and repatriation of POWs

After they surrendered, the Portuguese soldiers were interned by the Indian Army at their own military camps at Navelim, Aguada, Pondá and Alparqueiros under harsh conditions which included sleeping on cement floors and hard manual labour.[31] By January 1962, most POWs had been transferred to the newly established camp at Ponda where conditions were substantially better.[31]

Portuguese non-combatants present in Goa at the surrender—which included Mrs Vassalo e Silva, wife of the Portuguese Governor General of Goa—were transported by 29 December to Bombay, from where they were repatriated to Portugal. Manuel Vassalo e Silva, however, remained along with approximately 3,300 Portuguese combatants as POWs in Goa.

Air Marshal S. Raghavendran, who met some of the captured Portuguese soldiers, wrote in his memoirs several years later "I have never seen such a set of troops looking so miserable in my life. Short, not particularly well built and certainly very unsoldierlike."[69]

In one incident, recounted by Lieutenant Francisco Cabral Couto (now retired general), on 19 March 1962 some of the prisoners tried to escape the Ponda camp in a garbage truck. The attempt was foiled, and the Portuguese officers in charge of the escapees were threatened with court martial and execution by the Indians. This situation was defused by the timely intervention of Ferreira da Silva, a Jesuit military chaplain.[31][70] Following the foiled escape attempt, Captain Carlos Azeredo (now retired general) was beaten with rifle butts by four Indian soldiers while a gun was pointed at him, on the orders of Captain Naik, the 2nd Camp Commander. The beating was in retaliation for Azeredo's telling Captain Naik to "Go to Hell", and was serious enough to make him lose consciousness and cause severe contusions. Captain Naik was later punished by the Indian Army for violating the Geneva Convention.[15]

During the internment of the Portuguese POWs at various camps around Goa, the prisoners were visited by large numbers of Goans—described by Captain Azeredo as "Goan friends, acquaintances, or simply anonymous persons"—who offered the internees cigarettes, biscuits, tea, medicines and money. This surprised the Indian military authorities, who first limited the visits to twice a week, and then only to representatives of the Red Cross.[15]

The captivity lasted for six months "thanks to the stupid stubbornness of Lisbon" (according to Capt. Carlos Azeredo). The Portuguese Government insisted that the POWs be repatriated by Portuguese aircraft—a demand that was rejected by the Indian Government who instead insisted on aircraft from a neutral country. The negotiations were delayed even further when Salazar ordered the detention of 1200 Indians in Mozambique allegedly as a bargaining chip in exchange for Portuguese POWs.[15]

By May 1962, most of the POWs had been repatriated—being first flown to Karachi, Pakistan, in chartered French aircraft, and then sent off to Lisbon by three ships: *Vera Cruz*, *Pátria* and *Moçambique*.[71] On arrival at the Tejo in Portugal, returning Portuguese servicemen were taken into custody by military police at gunpoint without immediate access to their families who had arrived to receive them. Following intense questioning and interrogations, the officers were charged with direct insubordination on having refused to comply with directives not to surrender to the Indians. On 22 March 1963, the governor general, the military commander, his chief of staff, one naval captain, six majors, a sub lieutenant and a sergeant were cashiered by the council of ministers for cowardice and expelled from military service. Four captains, four lieutenants and a lieutenant commander were suspended for six months.[36]

Ex-governor Manuel António Vassalo e Silva had a hostile reception when he returned to Portugal. He was subsequently court martialed for failing to follow orders, expelled from the military and sent into exile. He returned to Portugal only in 1974, after the fall of the regime, and was given back his military status. He was later able to conduct a state visit to Goa, where he was given a warm reception.[72]

International reaction to the capture of Goa

Support

African states

Before the invasion the press speculated about international reaction to military action and recalled the recent charge by African nations that India was "too soft" on Portugal and was thus "dampening the enthusiasm of freedom fighters in other countries".[27] Many African countries, themselves former European colonies, reacted positively to the capture of Goa by the Indians. Radio Ghana termed it as the "Liberation of Goa" and went on to state that the people of Ghana would "long for the day when our downtrodden brethren in Angola and other Portuguese territories in Africa are liberated." Adelino Gwambe, the leader of the Mozambique National Democratic Union stated: "We fully support the use of force against Portuguese butchers."[27]

Also in 1961, the tiny Portuguese enclave of Fort of São João Baptista de Ajudá was annexed by the Republic of Dahomey (now Benin). Portugal recognised the annexation in 1975.[*citation needed*]

Soviet Union

The future leader of the Soviet Union, Leonid Brezhnev, who was touring India at the time of the war, made several speeches applauding the Indian action. In a farewell message, he urged Indians to ignore Western indignation as it came "from those who are accustomed to strangle the peoples striving for independence... and from those who enrich themselves from colonialist plunder". Nikita Khrushchev, the de facto Soviet leader, telegraphed Nehru stating that there was "unanimous acclaim" from every Soviet citizen for "Friendly India". The USSR had earlier vetoed a UN security council resolution condemning the Indian annexation of Goa.[73][74][75]

Arab States

The United Arab Republic expressed its full support for India's "legitimate efforts to regain its occupied territory". A Moroccan Government spokesman said that "India has been extraordinarily patient and a non-violent country has been driven to violence by Portugal"; while Tunisia's Secretary of State for Foreign Affairs of Tunisia, Sadok Mokaddem expressed the hope that "the liberation of Goa will bring nearer the end of the Portuguese colonial regime in Africa." Similar expressions of support for India were forthcoming from other Arab countries.[57]

Ceylon

Full support for India's action was expressed in Ceylon, where Prime Minister Sirimavo Bandaranaike issued an order on 18 December directing that "transport carrying troops and equipment for the Portuguese in Goa shall not be permitted the use of Ceylon's seaports and airports." Ceylon went on, along with delegates from Liberia and the UAR, to present a resolution in the UN in support of India's annexation of Goa.[57]

Condemnation

United States

The United States' official reaction to the annexation of Goa was delivered by Adlai Stevenson in the United Nations Security Council, where he condemned the armed action of the Indian government and demanded that all Indian forces be unconditionally withdrawn from Goan soil.

To express its displeasure with the Indian action in Goa, the US Senate Foreign Relations Committee attempted, over the objections of President John F. Kennedy, to cut the 1962 foreign aid appropriation to India by 25 percent.[76]

Referring to the perception, especially in the West, that India had previously been lecturing the world about the virtues of nonviolence, President Kennedy told the Indian ambassador to the US, "You spend the last fifteen years preaching morality to us, and then you go ahead and act the way any normal country would behave... People are saying, the preacher has been caught coming out of the brothel."[77]

In an article titled "India, The Aggressor", *The New York Times* on 19 December 1961, stated "With his invasion of Goa Prime Minister Nehru has done irreparable damage to India's good name and to the principles of international morality."[78]

Life International, in its issue dated 12 February 1962, carried an article titled "Symbolic pose by Goa's Governor" in which it expressed its vehement condemnation of the military action.

The world's initial outrage at pacifist India's resort to military violence for conquest has subsided into resigned disdain. And in Goa, a new Governor strikes a symbolic pose before portraits of men who had administered the prosperous Portuguese enclave for 451 years. He is K. P. Candeth, commanding India's 17th Infantry Division, and as the very model of a modern major general, he betrayed no sign that he is finding Goans less than happy about their "liberation". Goan girls refuse to dance with Indian officers. Goan shops have been stripped bare by luxury-hungry Indian soldiers, and Indian import restrictions prevent replacement. Even in India, doubts are heard. "India", said respected Chakravarti Rajagopalachari, leader of the Swatantra Party, "has totally lost the moral power to raise her voice against the use of military power"

— "Symbolic pose by Goa's Governor", Life International, 12 February 1962

United Kingdom

Commonwealth Relations Secretary, Duncan Sandys told the House of Commons on 18 December 1961 that while the UK Government had long understood the desire of the Indian people to incorporate Goa, Daman, and Diu in the Indian Republic, and their feeling of impatience that the Portuguese Government had not followed the example of Britain and France in relinquishing their Indian possessions, he had to "make it plain that H.M. Government deeply deplores the decision of the Government of India to use military force to attain its political objectives."

The Leader of the Opposition in the House of Commons Hugh Gaitskell of the Labour Party also expressed "profound regret" that India should have resorted to force in her dispute with Portugal, although the Opposition recognised that the existence of Portuguese colonies on the Indian mainland had long been an anachronism and that Portugal should have abandoned them long since in pursuance of the example set by Britain and France. Permanent Representative of the United Kingdom to the United Nations, Sir Patrick Dean, stated in the UN that Britain had been "shocked and dismayed" at the outbreak of hostilities.[57]

Netherlands

A Foreign Ministry spokesman in The Hague regretted that India, "of all countries," had resorted to force to gain her ends, particularly as India had always championed the principles of the U.N. Charter and consistently opposed the use of force to achieve national purposes. Fears were expressed in the Dutch Press lest the Indian attack on Goa might encourage Indonesia to make a similar attack on West New Guinea.[57] On 27 December 1961, Dutch ambassador to the United States, Herman Van Roijen asked the US Government if their military support in the form of the USN's 7th Fleet would be forthcoming in case of such an attack.[79]

Brazil

The Brazilian government's reaction to the annexation of Goa was one of staunch solidarity with Portugal, reflecting earlier statements by Brazilian presidents that their country stood firmly with Portugal anywhere in the world and that ties between Brazil and Portugal were built on ties of blood and sentiment. Former Brazilian President Juscelino Kubitschek, and long time friend and supporter of Portuguese PM Salazar, stated to Indian PM Nehru that "Seventy Million Brazilians could never understand, nor accept, an act of violence against Goa." [80] In a speech in Rio de Janeiro on 10 June 1962, Brazilian congressman Gilberto Freyre commented on the annexation of Goa by declaring that "a Portuguese wound is Brazilian pain".[81]

Shortly after the conflict, the new Brazilian ambassador to India, Mário Guimarães, stated to the Portuguese ambassador to Greece that it was "necessary for the Portuguese to comprehend that the age of colonialism is over". Guimarães dismissed the Portuguese ambassador's argument that Portuguese colonialism was based on miscegenation and the creation of multiracial societies, stating that this was "not enough of a reason to prevent independence".[82]

Pakistan

In a statement released on 18 December, the Pakistani Foreign Ministry spokesman described the Indian attack on Goa as "naked militarism". The statement emphasised that Pakistan stood for the settlement of international disputes by negotiation through the United Nations and stated that the proper course was a "U.N.-sponsored plebiscite to elicit from the people of Goa their wishes on the future of the territory." The Pakistani statement (issued on 18 December) continued: "The world now knows that India has double standards.... One set of principles seem to apply to India, another set to non-India. This is one more demonstration of the fact that India remains violent and aggressive at heart, whatever the pious statements made from time to time by its leaders."[57]

"The lesson from the Indian action on Goa is of practical interest on the question of Kashmir. Certainly the people of Kashmir could draw inspiration from what the Indians are reported to have stated in the leaflets they dropped...

on Goa. The leaflets stated that it was India's task to 'defend the honour and security of the Motherland from which the people of Goa had been separated far too long' and which the people of Goa, largely by their own efforts could again make their own. We hope the Indians will apply the same logic to Kashmir. Now the Indians can impress their electorate with having achieved military glory. The mask is off. Their much-proclaimed theories of non-violence, secularism, and democratic methods stand exposed."[57]

In a letter to the US President on 2 January 1962, Pakistani President General Ayub Khan stated: "My Dear President, The forcible taking of Goa by India has demonstrated what we in Pakistan have never had any illusions about—that India would not hesitate to attack if it were in her interest to do so and if she felt that the other side was too weak to resist."[83]

Ambivalence

People's Republic of China

In an official statement issued on 19 December, the Chinese government stressed its "resolute support" for the struggle of the people of Asia, Africa and Latin America against "imperialist colonialism". However, the Hong Kong Communist newspaper *Ta Kung Pao* (regarded as reflecting the views of the Peking Government) described the attack on Goa as "a desperate attempt by Mr. Nehru to regain his sagging prestige among the Afro-Asian nations." The *Ta Kung Pao* article – published before the statement from the Chinese Government – conceded that Goa was legitimately part of Indian territory and that the Indian people were entitled to take whatever measures were necessary to recover it. At the same time, however, the paper ridiculed Mr. Nehru for choosing "the world's tiniest imperialist country" to achieve his aim and asserted that "internal unrest, the failure of Nehru's anti-China campaign, and the forthcoming election forced him to take action against Goa to please the Indian people."[57]

The Catholic Church

The Roman Catholic Archbishop of Goa and Daman and Patriarch of the East Indies was always a Portuguese-born cleric; at the time of the annexation, José Vieira Alvernaz was archbishop, and days earlier Dom José Pedro da Silva had been nominated by the Holy See as coadjutor bishop with right to succeed Alvernaz. After the annexation, Silva remained in Portugal and was never consecrated; in 1965 he became bishop of Viseu in Portugal. Alvernaz retired to the Azores but remained titular Patriarch until resigning in 1975 after Portuguese recognition of the 1961 annexation.

Although the Vatican did not voice its reaction to the annexation of Goa, it delayed the appointment of a native head of the Goan Church until the inauguration of the Second Vatican Council in Rome, when Msgr Francisco Xavier da Piedade Rebelo was consecrated Bishop and Vicar Apostolic of Goa in 1963.[84][85] His was succeeded by Raul Nicolau Gonçalves in 1972, who became the first native-born Patriarch in 1978.[86]

Legality

Upon independence in 1947 India had accorded recognition to the Portuguese sovereignty over Goa. After invading Goa India's case was built around the illegality of colonial acquisitions. This argument was correct according to the legal norms of the twentieth century, but did not hold to the standards of sixteenth century international law. India gained sympathy from much of the international community, but this did not, however, signify any legal support for the invasion.[87] The Indian Supreme Court recognised the validity of the annexation and rejected the continued applicability of the law of occupation. In a treaty with retroactive effect, Portugal recognised Indian sovereignty in 1974.[88] Under the *jus cogens* rule forceful annexations including the annexation of Goa are held as illegal since they have taken place after the UN Charter came into force. A later treaty can not justify it.[89] Sharon Korman argues that the principle of self-determination may bend the rule to accommodate the new reality but it will not change the illegal aspect of the original annexation.[90]

Cultural depiction

The movie *Saat Hindustani* (1969), was about Operation Vijay. It won the 1970 Nargis Dutt Award for Best Feature Film on National Integration, and the Lyric-Writer of the Best Film Song on National Integration Award for Kaifi Azmi. *Trikal*, a film by Shyam Benegal and Pukar also have storylines based on the backdrop of 1960s Goa.

CH 3 Kargil War

Kargil War

"Operation Vijay (1999)" redirects here. For the 1961 Indian operation, see Annexation of Goa.

Kargil War

Part of the Indo-Pakistani wars and conflicts and the Kashmir conflict

Indian soldiers in Batalik during

the Kargil War.jpg

Indian soldiers in Batalik during the war

Date

3 May – 26 July 1999

(2 months, 3 weeks and 2 days)

Location

Kargil district, Jammu and Kashmir, India

Result

Decisive Indian victory[1][2][3][4][5]

- India regains possession of Kargil

Territorial changes

None

Belligerents

India

Pakistan

Commanders and leaders

K. R. Narayanan
(President of India)
Atal Bihari Vajpayee
(Prime Minister of India)
Gen Ved Prakash Malik
(Chief of the Army Staff)
Lt Gen Chandra Shekhar
(Vice Chief of the Army Staff)
ACM Anil Yashwant Tipnis

Force
Ensign
of
India.svg

(Chief of the Air Staff)
Muhammad Rafiq Tarar
(President of Pakistan)
Nawaz Sharif
(Prime Minister of Pakistan)
Gen Pervez Musharraf
(Chief of the Army Staff)
Lt Gen Muhammad Aziz Khan
(Chief of the General Staff)
ACM Pervaiz Mehdi Qureshi
(Chief of the Air Staff)

Ensign
of
Pakistan.svg

Strength

30,000
5,000

Casualties and losses

Indian official figures

- 527 killed[6][7][8]
- 1,363 wounded[9]
- 1 POW
- 1 fighter jet shot down
- 1 fighter jet crashed
- 1 helicopter shot down

Pakistani claims

- 1,600 (as claimed by Musharraf)[10]

Independent figures

- 700 casualties[11]

Pakistani figures

- 453 killed (Pakistan army claim)[12][13]

Other Pakistani claims

- 357 killed and 665+ wounded (according to Pervez Musharraf)[14][15]
- 2,700–4,000 killed (according to Nawaz Sharif)[11][16]

Indian claims

- 737–1,200 casualties[17][18][19]
- 1,000+ wounded[20]

show

- v
- t
- e

Kargil War

show

- v
- t
- e

<u>Indo-Pakistani conflicts</u>

The **Kargil War**, also known as the **Kargil conflict**,[note (1)] was an <u>armed conflict</u> between <u>India</u> and <u>Pakistan</u> that took place between May and July 1999 in the <u>Kargil district</u> of <u>Kashmir</u> and elsewhere along the <u>Line of Control</u> (LOC). In India, the conflict is also referred to as **Operation Vijay** (<u>Hindi</u>: वजिय, literally "Victory") which was the name of the Indian operation to clear the Kargil sector.[21] The <u>Indian Air Force</u>'s role in acting jointly with <u>Ground troops</u> during the War that was aimed at flushing out Regular and Irregular troops of the <u>Pakistani Army</u> from vacated Indian Positions in the <u>Kargil</u> sector along the <u>Line of Control</u>.[22] was given the <u>code name</u> **Operation Safed Sagar** (<u>Hindi</u>: ऑपरेशन सफेद सागर, lit. "Operation White Sea")

The cause of the war was the infiltration of Pakistani soldiers disguised as Kashmiri militants into positions on the Indian side of the LOC,[23] which serves as the *de facto* border between the two states. During the initial stages of the war, Pakistan blamed the fighting entirely on independent Kashmiri insurgents, but documents left behind by <u>casualties</u> and later statements by Pakistan's <u>Prime Minister</u> and <u>Chief of Army Staff</u> showed involvement of Pakistani paramilitary forces,[24][25][26] led by General <u>Ashraf Rashid</u>.[27] The <u>Indian Army</u>, later supported by the <u>Indian Air Force</u>, recaptured a majority of the positions on the Indian side of the LOC infiltrated by the Pakistani troops and militants. Facing international diplomatic opposition, the Pakistani forces withdrew from the remaining Indian positions along the LOC.

The war is one of the most recent examples of <u>high-altitude warfare in mountainous terrain</u>, which posed significant <u>logistical problems</u> for the combating sides. It is also one of the very few instances of direct, <u>conventional warfare</u> between <u>nuclear states</u> (i.e., those possessing <u>nuclear weapons</u>). India had conducted its first successful test <u>in 1974</u>; Pakistan, which had been developing its <u>nuclear capability</u> in secret since around the same time, conducted its first known tests <u>in 1998</u>, just two weeks after a <u>second series of tests</u> by India.

Contents

Location

Location of the conflict

Before the Partition of India in 1947, Kargil was a tehsil of Ladakh, a sparsely populated region with diverse linguistic, ethnic and religious groups, living in isolated valleys separated by some of the world's highest mountains. The Indo-Pakistani War of 1947-1948 concluded with the Line of Control bisecting the Ladakh district, with the Skardu tehsil going to Pakistan (now part of Gilgit-Baltistan).[28] After Pakistan's defeat in the Indo-Pakistani War of 1971, the two nations signed the Simla Agreement promising not to engage in armed conflict with respect to that boundary.[29]

The town of Kargil is located 205 km (127 mi) from Srinagar, facing the Northern Areas across the LOC.[30] Like other areas in the Himalayas, Kargil has a continental climate. Summers are cool with frigid nights, while winters are long and chilly with temperatures often dropping to −48 °C (−54 °F).[31]

An Indian national highway (NH 1) connecting Srinagar to Leh cuts through Kargil. The area that witnessed the infiltration and fighting is a 160-kilometre (100 mi) long stretch of ridges overlooking this only road linking Srinagar and Leh.[23] The military outposts on the ridges above the highway were generally around 5,000 m (16,000 ft) high, with a few as high as 5,485 m (18,000 ft).[32] Apart from the district capital, Kargil, the populated areas near the front line in the conflict included the Mushko Valley and the town of Drass, southwest of Kargil, as well as the Batalik sector and other areas, northeast of Kargil.

Kargil was targeted partly because the terrain was conducive to the preemptive seizure of several unoccupied military positions.[33] With tactically vital features and well-prepared defensive posts atop the peaks, a defender on the high ground would enjoy advantages akin to a fortress. Any attack to dislodge a defender from high ground in mountain warfare requires a far higher ratio of attackers to defenders,[34] and the difficulties would be exacerbated by the high altitude and freezing temperatures.[35]

Kargil is just 173 km (107 mi) from the Pakistani-controlled town of Skardu, which was capable of providing logistical and artillery support to Pakistani combatants. A road between Kargil and Skardu exists, which was closed in 1949.[36]

Background

The town of Kargil is strategically located.

After the Indo-Pakistani War of 1971, there had been a long period with relatively few direct armed conflicts involving the military forces of the two neighbours – notwithstanding the efforts of both nations to control the Siachen Glacier by establishing military outposts on the surrounding mountains ridges and the resulting military skirmishes in the 1980s.[37] During the 1990s, however, escalating tensions and conflict due to separatist activities in Kashmir, some of which were supported by Pakistan,[38][39][40][41][42][43][44] as well as the conducting of nuclear tests by both countries in 1998, led to an increasingly belligerent atmosphere. In an attempt to defuse the situation, both countries signed the Lahore Declaration in February 1999, promising to provide a peaceful and bilateral solution to the Kashmir conflict.

During the winter of 1998–1999, some elements of the Pakistani Armed Forces were covertly training and sending Pakistani troops and paramilitary forces, some allegedly in the guise of mujahideen, into territory on the Indian side of the LOC. The infiltration was codenamed "Operation Badr";[45][46][47] its aim was to sever the link between Kashmir and Ladakh, and cause Indian forces to withdraw from the Siachen Glacier, thus forcing India to negotiate a settlement of the broader Kashmir dispute. Pakistan also believed that any tension in the region would internationalise the Kashmir issue, helping it to secure a speedy resolution. Yet another goal may have been to boost the morale of the decade-long rebellion in Jammu and Kashmir by taking a proactive role.

Pakistani Lieutenant General Shahid Aziz, and then head of ISI analysis wing, has confirmed there were no mujahideen but only regular Pakistan Army soldiers who took part in the Kargil War.[48] "There were no Mujahideen, only taped wireless messages, which fooled no one. Our soldiers were made to occupy barren ridges, with hand held weapons and ammunition", Lt Gen Aziz wrote in his article in *The Nation* daily in January 2013.[49]

Some writers have speculated that the operation's objective may also have been retaliation for India's Operation Meghdoot in 1984 that seized much of Siachen Glacier.[50]

According to India's then army chief Ved Prakash Malik, and many scholars,[51][52] much of the background planning, including construction of logistical supply routes, had been undertaken much earlier. On several occasions during the 1980s and 1990s, the army had given Pakistani leaders (Zia ul Haq and Benazir Bhutto) similar proposals for infiltration into the Kargil region, but the plans had been shelved for fear of drawing the nations into all-out war.[53][54][55]

Some analysts believe that the blueprint of attack was reactivated soon after Pervez Musharraf was appointed chief of army staff in October 1998.[45][56] After the war, Nawaz Sharif, Prime Minister of Pakistan during the Kargil conflict, claimed that he was unaware of the plans, and that he first learned about the situation when he received an urgent phone call from Atal Bihari Vajpayee, his counterpart in India.[57] Sharif attributed the plan to Musharraf and "just two or three of his cronies",[58] a view shared by some Pakistani writers who have stated that only four generals, including Musharraf, knew of the plan.[53][59] Musharraf, however, asserted that Sharif had been briefed on the Kargil operation 15 days ahead of Vajpayee's journey to Lahore on 20 February.[60]

War progress

Further information: Kargil order of battle

Conflict events

Date (1999)

Event[61][62][63]

3 May
Pakistani intrusion in Kargil reported by local shepherds.
5 May
Indian Army patrol sent up; 5 Indian soldiers captured and tortured to death.
9 May
Heavy shelling by Pakistan Army damages ammunition dump in Kargil.
10 May
Infiltrations first noticed in Dras, Kaksar, and Mushkoh sectors.
Mid-May
Indian Army moves in more troops from Kashmir Valley to Kargil Sector.
26 May
IAF launches air strikes against infiltrators.
27 May
IAF loses a MiG-21 and a MiG-27; Flt. Lt. Kambampati Nachiketa taken POW.
28 May
IAF MI-17 shot down by Pakistan; four air crew dead.
1 June
Pakistan steps up attacks; shells NH 1.

5 June

Indian Army releases documents recovered from three Pakistani soldiers indicating Pakistan's involvement.

6 June

Indian Army launches major offensive in Kargil.

9 June

Indian Army re-captures two key positions in the Batalik sector.

11 June

India releases intercepts of conversation between Pakistan Army Chief Gen. Pervez Musharraf, while on a visit to China and Chief of General Staff Lt. Gen. Aziz Khan in Rawalpindi, as proof of Pakistan Army's involvement.

13 June

Indian Army secures Tololing in Dras.

15 June

U.S. President Bill Clinton, in a telephonic conversation, asks Pakistani Prime Minister Nawaz Sharif to pull out from Kargil.

29 June

Indian Army captures Point 5060 and Point 5100, two vital posts near Tiger Hill.

2 July

Indian Army launches three-pronged attack in Kargil.

4 July

Indian Army recaptures Tiger Hill after an 11-hour battle.

5 July

Indian Army takes control of Dras. Sharif announces Pakistan Army's withdrawal from Kargil following his meeting with Clinton.

7 July

India recaptures Jubar Heights in Batalik.

11 July

Pakistan begins pullout; India captures key peaks in Batalik.

14 July

Indian Prime Minister Atal Bihari Vajpayee declares Operation Vijay a success. Government sets condition for talks with Pakistan.

26 July

Kargil conflict officially comes to an end. Indian Army announces complete eviction of Pakistani intruders.

There were three major phases to the Kargil War. First, Pakistan infiltrated forces into the Indian-controlled section of Kashmir and occupied strategic locations enabling it to bring NH1 within range of its artillery fire. The next stage consisted of India discovering the infiltration and mobilising forces to respond to it. The final stage involved major battles by Indian and Pakistani forces resulting in India recapturing most of the territories[64][65] held by Pakistani forces and the subsequent withdrawal of Pakistani forces back across the LOC after international pressure.

Occupation by Pakistan

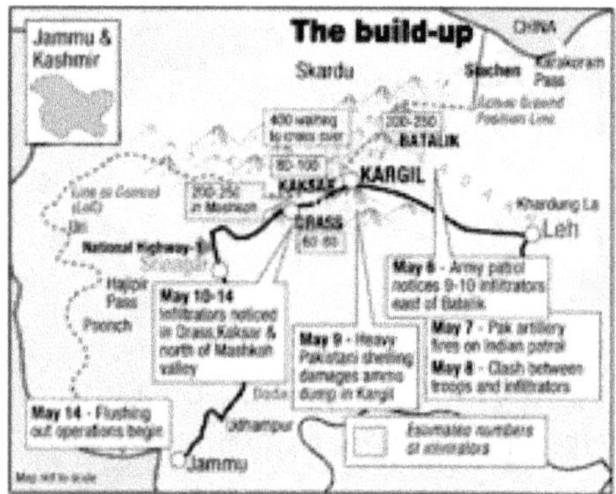

Infiltration and military build-up

During February 1999, the Pakistan Army sent forces to occupy some posts on the Indian side of the LOC.[66] Troops from the elite Special Services Group as well as four to seven battalions[67][68] of the Northern Light Infantry (a paramilitary regiment not part of the regular Pakistani army at that time) covertly and overtly set up bases on 132 vantage points of the Indian-controlled region.[69] According to some reports, these Pakistani forces were backed by Kashmiri guerrillas and Afghan mercenaries.[70] According to General Ved Malik, the bulk of the infiltration occurred in April 1999.[71]

Pakistani intrusions took place in the heights of the lower Mushkoh Valley, along the Marpo La ridgeline in Dras, in Kaksar near Kargil, in the Batalik sector east of the Indus River, on the heights above of the Chorbatla sector where the LOC turns North and in the Turtok sector south of the Siachen area.

India discovers infiltration and mobilises

Initially, these incursions were not detected for a number of reasons: Indian patrols were not sent into some of the areas infiltrated by the Pakistani forces and heavy artillery fire by Pakistan in some areas provided cover for the infiltrators. But by the second week of May, the ambushing of an Indian patrol team led by Capt Saurabh Kalia, who acted on a tip-off by a local shepherd in the Batalik sector, led to the exposure of the infiltration.[72] Initially, with little knowledge of the nature or extent of the infiltration, the Indian troops in the area assumed that the infiltrators were jihadis and claimed that they would evict them within a few days. Subsequent discovery of infiltration elsewhere along the LOC, and the difference in tactics employed by the infiltrators, caused the Indian army to realise that the plan of attack was on a much bigger scale. The total area seized by the ingress is generally accepted to between 130 and 200 km² (50 and 80 sq mi).[59][67][73]

The Government of India responded with Operation Vijay, a mobilisation of 200,000 Indian troops. However, because of the nature of the terrain, division and corps operations could not be mounted; subsequent fighting was conducted mostly at the brigade or battalion level. In effect, two divisions of the Indian Army,[74] numbering 20,000, plus several thousand from the Paramilitary forces of India and the air force were deployed in the conflict zone. The total number of Indian soldiers that were involved in the military operation on the Kargil-Drass sector was thus close to 30,000. The number of infiltrators, including those providing logistical backup, has been put at approximately 5,000 at the height of the conflict.[23][59][70] This figure includes troops from Pakistan-administered Kashmir who provided additional artillery support.

The Indian Air Force launched Operation Safed Sagar in support of the mobilisation of Indian land forces on May 26. The Indian Govt cleared limited use of Air Power only on May 25, for fear of undesirable escalation, with the fiat that IAF fighter jets were not to cross the LOC under any circumstance.[75] This was the first time any air war was fought at such high altitudes globally, with targets between 6-18,000' AMSL. The rarified air at these altitudes affected ballistic trajectories of air to ground weapons, such as rockets, dumb and laser guided bombs. There was no opposition at all by the Pakistani Air Force, leaving the IAF free to carry out its attacks with impunity.[76][77] The total air dominance of the IAF gave the aircrew enough time to modify aiming indices and firing techniques, increasing its effectiveness during the high altitude war. Poor weather conditions and range limitations intermittently affected bomb loads and the number of <u>airstrips</u> that could be used, except for the Mirage 2000 fleet, which commenced operations on May 30.[78]

Naval action

The <u>Indian Navy</u> also prepared to blockade the <u>Pakistani ports</u> (primarily the <u>Karachi port</u>)[79] to cut off supply routes under *Operation Talwar*.[80][81][82][83] The Indian Navy's <u>western</u> and <u>eastern fleets</u> joined in the North <u>Arabian Sea</u> and began aggressive patrols and threatened to cut Pakistan's sea trade. This exploited Pakistan's dependence on sea-based oil and trade flows.[84] Later, then-<u>Prime Minister of Pakistan</u>, Nawaz Sharif disclosed that Pakistan was left with just six days of fuel to sustain itself if a full-scale war had broken out.[23][85][86][87]

India attacks Pakistani positions

This section **needs additional citations for** <u>verification</u>. Please help <u>improve this article</u> by <u>adding citations to reliable sources</u>. Unsourced material may be challenged and removed.
Find sources: <u>"Kargil War"</u> – <u>news</u> · <u>newspapers</u> · <u>books</u> · <u>scholar</u> · <u>JSTOR</u> *(July 2017) (*<u>*Learn how and when to remove this template message*</u>*)*

The terrain of Kashmir is mountainous and at high altitudes; even the best roads, such as <u>National Highway 1 (India)</u> (NH1) from Srinagar to Leh, are only two lanes. The rough terrain and narrow roads slowed down traffic, and the high altitude, which affected the ability of aircraft to carry loads, made control of NH 1 (the actual stretch of the highway which was under Pakistani fire) a priority for India. From their 130+ covertly occupied <u>observation posts</u>, the Pakistani forces had a clear line-of-sight to lay down <u>indirect artillery fire</u> on NH 1, inflicting heavy casualties on the Indians.[88] This was a serious problem for the Indian Army as the highway was the main logistical and supply route.[89] The Pakistani shelling of the <u>arterial road</u> posed the threat of Leh being cut off, though an alternative (and longer) road to Leh existed via <u>Himachal Pradesh</u>, the <u>Leh–Manali Highway</u>.

Indian soldiers after winning a battle during the Kargil War

The infiltrators, apart from being equipped with <u>small arms</u> and <u>grenade launchers</u>, were also armed with <u>mortars</u>, <u>artillery</u> and <u>anti-aircraft guns</u>.[90] Many posts were also heavily <u>mined</u>, with India later stating to have recovered more than 8,000 <u>anti-personnel mines</u> according to an <u>ICBL</u> report.[91] Pakistan's <u>reconnaissance</u> was done through <u>unmanned aerial vehicles</u> and <u>AN/TPQ-36 Firefinder radars</u> supplied by the US.[92] The initial Indian attacks were aimed at controlling the hills overlooking NH 1, with high priority being given to the stretches of the highway near the town of Kargil. The majority of posts along the LOC were adjacent to the highway, and therefore the recapture of nearly every infiltrated post increased both the territorial gains and the security of the highway. The protection of this route and the recapture of the forward posts were thus ongoing objectives throughout the war.

The Indian Army's first priority was to recapture peaks that were in the immediate vicinity of NH 1. This resulted in Indian troops first targeting the Tiger Hill and Tololing complex in Dras, which dominated the Srinagar-Leh route.[93] This was soon followed by the Batalik-Turtok sub-sector which provided access to Siachen Glacier. Some of the peaks that were of vital strategic importance to the Pakistani defensive troops were Point 4590 and Point 5353. While 4590 was the nearest point that had a view of NH 1, point 5353 was the highest feature in the Dras sector, allowing the Pakistani troops to observe NH 1.[94] The recapture of Point 4590 by Indian troops on 14 June was significant, notwithstanding the fact that it resulted in the Indian Army suffering the most casualties in a single battle during the conflict.[95] Though most of the posts in the vicinity of the highway were cleared by mid-June, some parts of the highway near Drass witnessed sporadic shelling until the end of the war.

IAF MiG-21s were used extensively in the Kargil War.

Once India regained control of the hills overlooking NH 1, the Indian Army turned to driving the invading force back across the LOC. The Battle of Tololing, amongst other assaults, slowly tilted the combat in India's favour. The Pakistani troops at Tololing were aided by Pakistani fighters from Kashmir. Some of the posts put up a stiff resistance, including Tiger Hill (Point 5140) that fell only later in the war. Indian troops found well-entrenched Pakistani soldiers at Tiger Hill, and both sides suffered heavy casualties. After a final assault on the peak in which ten Pakistani soldiers and five Indian soldiers were killed, Tiger Hill finally fell. A few of the assaults occurred atop hitherto unheard of peaks – most of them unnamed with only Point numbers to differentiate them – which witnessed fierce hand to hand combat.

As the operation was fully underway, about 250 artillery guns were brought in to clear the infiltrators in the posts that were in the line-of-sight. The Bofors FH-77B field howitzer played a vital role, with Indian gunners making maximum use of the terrain. However, its success was limited elsewhere due to the lack of space and depth to deploy it.

The Indian Air Force was tasked to act jointly with ground troops on 25 May.[75] The code name assigned to their role was Operation Safed Sagar [96] It was in this type of terrain that aerial attacks were used, initially with limited effectiveness. On 27 May 1999, the IAF lost a MiG-27 strike aircraft piloted by Flt. Lt. Nachiketa, which it attributed to an engine failure, and a MiG-21 fighter piloted by Sqn Ldr Ajay Ahuja which was shot down by the Pakistani army, both over Batalik sector.;[97][98] initially Pakistan said it shot down both jets after they crossed into its territory.[99] According to reports, Ahuja had bailed out of his stricken plane safely but was apparently killed by his captors as his body was returned riddled with bullet wounds.[23] One Indian Mi-8 helicopter was also lost due to Stinger SAMs. French made Mirage 2000H of the IAF were tasked to drop laser-guided bombs to destroy well-entrenched positions of the Pakistani forces [23] and flew its first sortie on May 30.[100] The effects of the pinpoint non-stop bombing by the Mirage-2000, by day and by night, became evident with almost immediate effect.[101]

In many vital points, neither artillery nor air power could dislodge the outposts manned by the Pakistani soldiers, who were out of visible range. The Indian Army mounted some direct frontal ground assaults which were slow and took a heavy toll given the steep ascent that had to be made on peaks as high as 5,500 metres (18,000 ft). Since any daylight attack would be suicidal, all the advances had to be made under the cover of darkness, escalating the risk of freezing. Accounting for the wind chill factor, the temperatures were often as low as −15 to −11 °C (5 to 12 °F) near the mountain tops. Based on military tactics, much of the costly frontal assaults by the Indians could have been avoided if the Indian Military had chosen to blockade the supply route of the opposing force, creating a siege. Such a move would have involved the Indian troops crossing the LOC as well as initiating aerial attacks on Pakistani soil, a manoeuvre India was not willing to exercise fearing an expansion of the theatre of war and reduced international support for its cause.

Two months into the conflict, Indian troops had slowly retaken most of the ridges that were encroached upon by the infiltrators;[64][65] according to the official count, an estimated 75–80% of the intruded area and nearly all the high ground were back under Indian control.[45]

Withdrawal and final battles

Following the outbreak of armed fighting, Pakistan sought American help in de-escalating the conflict. Bruce Riedel, who was then an aide to President Bill Clinton, reported that US intelligence had imaged Pakistani movements of nuclear weapons to forward deployments for fear of the Kargil hostilities escalating into a wider conflict. However, President Clinton refused to intervene until Pakistan had removed all forces from the Indian side of the LOC.[102] Following the Washington accord of 4 July 1999, when Sharif agreed to withdraw Pakistani troops, most of the fighting came to a gradual halt, but some Pakistani forces remained in positions on the Indian side of the LOC. In addition, the United Jihad Council (an umbrella for extremist groups) rejected Pakistan's plan for a climb-down, instead deciding to fight on.[103]

The Indian army launched its final attacks in the last week of July in co-ordination with relentless attacks by the IAF, both by day and night, in their totally successful Operation Safed Sagar; as soon as the Drass subsector had been cleared of Pakistani forces, the fighting ceased on 26 July. The day has since been marked as *Kargil Vijay Diwas* (Kargil Victory Day) in India. By the end of the war, Pakistan had to withdraw under international pressure and due to pressure from continued fighting at battle front and left India in control of all territory south and east of the LOC, as was established in July 1972 as per the Simla Agreement.[104]

World opinion

Pakistan was heavily criticised by other countries for instigating the war, as its paramilitary forces and insurgents crossed the LOC (Line of Control).[105] Pakistan's primary diplomatic response, one of plausible deniability linking the incursion to what it officially termed as "Kashmiri freedom fighters", was in the end not successful.[106] Veteran analysts argued that the battle was fought at heights where only seasoned troops could survive, so poorly equipped "freedom fighters" would neither have the ability nor the wherewithal to seize land and defend it. Moreover, while the army had initially denied the involvement of its troops in the intrusion, two soldiers were awarded the Nishan-E-Haider (Pakistan's highest military honour). Another 90 soldiers were also given gallantry awards, most of them posthumously, confirming Pakistan's role in the episode. India also released taped phone conversations between the Army Chief and a senior Pakistani general where the latter is recorded saying: "the scruff of [the militants] necks is in our hands",[107] although Pakistan dismissed it as a "total fabrication". Concurrently, Pakistan made several contradicting statements, confirming its role in Kargil, when it defended the incursions saying that the LOC itself was disputed.[108] Pakistan also attempted to internationalise the Kashmir issue, by linking the crisis in Kargil to the larger Kashmir conflict, but such a diplomatic stance found few backers on the world stage.[109]

As the Indian counter-attacks picked up momentum, Pakistani prime minister Nawaz Sharif flew to meet US President Bill Clinton on 4 July to obtain support from the United States. Clinton rebuked Sharif, however, and asked him to use his contacts to rein in the militants and withdraw Pakistani soldiers from Indian territory. Clinton would later reveal in his autobiography that "Sharif's moves were perplexing" since the Indian Prime Minister had travelled to Lahore to promote bilateral talks aimed at resolving the Kashmir problem and "by crossing the Line of Control, Pakistan had wrecked the [bilateral] talks".[110] On the other hand, he applauded Indian restraint for not crossing the LOC and escalating the conflict into an all-out war.[111]

G8 nations supported India and condemned the Pakistani violation of the LOC at the Cologne summit. The European Union also opposed Pakistan's violation of the LOC.[112] China, a long-time ally of Pakistan, insisted on a pullout of forces to the pre-conflict positions along the LOC and settling border issues peacefully. Other organisations like the ASEAN Regional Forum too supported India's stand on the inviolability of the LOC.[109]

Faced with growing international pressure, Sharif managed to pull back the remaining soldiers from Indian territory. The joint statement issued by Clinton and Sharif conveyed the need to respect the LOC and resume bilateral talks as the best forum to resolve all disputes.[113][114]

Gallantry awards

India

A number of Indian soldiers earned awards for gallantry:[115]

- Gren. Yogendra Singh Yadav, 18th Battalion, The Grenadiers: Param Vir Chakra
- Lt. Manoj Kumar Pandey, 1st Battalion, 11th Gorkha Rifles: Param Vir Chakra (posthumous)
- Capt. Vikram Batra, 13th Battalion, Jammu & Kashmir Rifles: Param Vir Chakra (posthumous)
- Rfn. Sanjay Kumar, 13th Battalion, Jammu and Kashmir Rifles: Param Vir Chakra
- Capt. Anuj Nayyar, 17th Battalion, Jat Regiment: Maha Vir Chakra (posthumous)
- Maj. Rajesh Singh Adhikari, 18th Battalion, The Grenadiers: Maha Vir Chakra (posthumous)
- Nk. Digendra Kumar, 2nd Battalion, Rajputana Rifles: Maha Vir Chakra
- Capt. Haneef Uddin, 11th Battalion, Rajputana Rifles: Vir Chakra (posthumous)
- Maj. Mariappan Saravanan, 1st Battalion, Bihar Regiment: Vir Chakra (posthumous)
- Sqn. Ldr. Ajay Ahuja, Indian Air Force: Vir Chakra (posthumous)
- Hav. Chuni Lal, 8th Battalion, Jammu and Kashmir Light Infantry: Vir Chakra
- Col. Magod Basappa Ravindranath, 2nd Battalion, Rajputana Rifles: Vir Chakra

Pakistan

Two Pakistani soldiers received the Nishan-e-Haider, Pakistan's highest military gallantry award:[116]

- Capt. Karnal Sher Khan, 27th Battalion, Sind Regiment: Nishan-e-Haider (posthumous)
- Hav. Lalak Jan, Northern Light Infantry: Nishan-e-Haider (posthumous)

Impact and influence of media

The Kargil War was significant for the impact and influence of the mass media on public opinion in both nations. Coming at a time of exploding growth in electronic journalism in India, the Kargil news stories and war footage were often telecast live on TV, and many websites provided in-depth analysis of the war.[117] The conflict became the first "live" war in South Asia and it was given such detailed media coverage that one effect was the drumming up of jingoistic feelings.[118]

The conflict soon turned into a news propaganda war, in which press briefings given by government officials of each nation produced conflicting claims and counterclaims. The Indian government placed a temporary News Embargo on information from Pakistan, banning the telecast of the state-run Pakistani channel PTV[119] and blocking access to online editions of the *Dawn* newspaper.[120] The Pakistani media criticised this apparent curbing of freedom of the press in India, while India media claimed it was in the interest of national security. The Indian government ran advertisements in foreign publications including *The Times* and *The Washington Post* detailing Pakistan's role in supporting extremists in Kashmir in an attempt to garner political support for its position.

As the war progressed, media coverage of the conflict was more intense in India than in Pakistan.[121] Many Indian channels showed images from the battle zone in a style reminiscent of CNN's coverage of the Gulf War (one of the shells fired by Pakistan troops even hit a Doordarshan transmission centre in Kargil while coverage continued).[122] Reasons for India's increased coverage included the greater number of privately owned electronic media in India compared to Pakistan and relatively greater transparency in the Indian media. At a seminar in Karachi, Pakistani journalists agreed that while the Indian government had taken the press and the people into its confidence, Pakistan had not.[123]

The print media in India and abroad was largely sympathetic to the Indian cause, with editorials in newspapers based in the west and other neutral countries observing that Pakistan was largely responsible for the conflict. Some analysts believe that Indian media, which was both larger in number and more credible, may have acted as a force multiplier for the Indian military operation in Kargil and served as a morale booster.[6][124] As the fighting intensified, the Pakistani version of events found little backing on the world stage. This helped India gain valuable diplomatic recognition for its position.

WMDs and the nuclear factor

Since Pakistan and India each had weapons of mass destruction, many in the international community were concerned that if the Kargil conflict intensified, it could lead to nuclear war. Both countries had tested their nuclear capability in 1998 (India conducted its first test in 1974 while it was Pakistan's first-ever nuclear test). Many pundits believed the tests to be an indication of the escalating stakes in the scenario in South Asia. When the Kargil conflict started just a year after the nuclear tests, many nations desired to end it before it intensified.

International concerns increased when Pakistani foreign secretary Shamshad Ahmad made a statement on 31 May warning that an escalation of the limited conflict could lead Pakistan to use "any weapon" in its arsenal.[125] This was immediately interpreted as a threat of nuclear retaliation by Pakistan in the event of an extended war, and the belief was reinforced when the leader of Pakistan's senate noted, "The purpose of developing weapons becomes meaningless if they are not used when they are needed".[126] Many such ambiguous statements from officials of both countries were viewed as warnings of an impending nuclear crisis where the combatants would consider use of their limited nuclear arsenals in "tactical" nuclear warfare in the belief that it would not have ended in mutual assured destruction, as could have occurred in a nuclear conflict between the United States and the USSR. Some experts believe that following nuclear tests in 1998, the Pakistani military was emboldened by its nuclear deterrent to markedly increase coercion against India.[127]

The nature of the India-Pakistan conflict took a more sinister turn when the United States received intelligence that Pakistani nuclear warheads were being moved towards the border. Bill Clinton tried to dissuade Pakistan prime minister Nawaz Sharif from nuclear brinkmanship, even threatening Pakistan of dire consequences. According to a White House official, Sharif seemed to be genuinely surprised by this supposed missile movement and responded that India was probably planning the same. In a May 2000 article, Sanjay Badri-Maharaj claimed that India too had readied at least five nuclear-tipped ballistic missiles, but could not back up this claim with any official proof.[128]

Sensing a deteriorating military scenario, diplomatic isolation, and the risks of a larger conventional and nuclear war, Sharif ordered the Pakistani army to vacate the Kargil heights. He later claimed in his official biography that General Pervez Musharraf had moved nuclear warheads without informing him.[129] Recently however, Pervez Musharraf revealed in his memoirs that Pakistan's nuclear delivery system was not operational during the Kargil war;[67] something that would have put Pakistan under serious disadvantage if the conflict went nuclear.

The threat of WMD included chemical and even biological weapons. Pakistan accused India of using chemical weapons and incendiary weapons such as napalm against the Kashmiri fighters. India, on the other hand, showcased a cache of gas masks as proof that Pakistan may have been prepared to use non-conventional weapons. US official and the Organisation for the Prohibition of Chemical Weapons determined that Pakistani allegations of India using banned chemicals in its bombs were unfounded.[130]

Aftermath

India

From the end of the war until February 2000, the Indian stock market rose by more than 30%. The next Indian national budget included major increases in military spending.

There was a surge in patriotism, with many celebrities expressing their support for the Kargil cause.[131] Indians were angered by media reports of the death of pilot Ajay Ahuja, especially after Indian authorities reported that Ahuja had been murdered and his body mutilated by Pakistani troops. The war had produced higher than expected fatalities for the Indian military, with a sizeable percentage of them including newly commissioned officers. One month after conclusion of the Kargil War, the Atlantique Incident, in which a Pakistan Navy plane was shot down by India, briefly reignited fears of a conflict between the two countries.

After the war, the Indian government severed ties with Pakistan and increased defence preparedness. India increased its defence budget as it sought to acquire more state of the art equipment.[132] Media reported about military procurement irregularities[133] and criticism of intelligence agencies like Research and Analysis Wing, which failed to predict the intrusions or the identity/number of infiltrators during the war. An internal assessment report by the armed forces, published in an Indian magazine, showed several other failings, including "a sense of complacency" and being "unprepared for a conventional war" on the presumption that nuclearism would sustain peace. It also highlighted the lapses in command and control, the insufficient troop levels and the dearth of large-calibre guns like the Bofors.[134] In 2006, retired Air Chief Marshal, A. Y. Tipnis, alleged that the Indian Army did not fully inform the government about the intrusions, adding that the army chief Ved Prakash Malik, was initially reluctant to use the full strike capability of the Indian Air Force, instead requesting only helicopter gunship support.[135] Soon after the conflict, India also decided to complete the project, previously stalled by Pakistan, to fence the entire LOC.[136]

The end of the Kargil conflict was followed by the 13th Indian General Elections to the Lok Sabha, which gave a decisive mandate to the National Democratic Alliance (NDA) government. It was re-elected to power in September–October 1999 with a majority of 303 seats out of 545 in the Lok Sabha. On the diplomatic front, Indo-US relations improved, as the United States appreciated Indian attempts to restrict the conflict to a limited geographic area.[137] Relations with Israel—which had discreetly aided India with ordnance supply and matériel such as unmanned aerial vehicles, laser-guided bombs, and satellite imagery—also were bolstered.[138]

Kargil Review Committee

Main article: Kargil Review Committee

Soon after the war the Atal Bihari Vajpayee government set up an inquiry into its causes and to analyse perceived Indian intelligence failures. The high-powered committee was chaired by eminent strategic affairs analyst K. Subrahmanyam and given powers to interview anyone with current or past associations with Indian security, including former Prime Ministers. The committee's final report (also referred to as the "Subrahmanyam Report")[139] led to a large-scale restructuring of Indian Intelligence.[140] It, however, came in for heavy criticism in the Indian media for its perceived avoidance of assigning specific responsibility for failures over detecting the Kargil intrusions.[141] The Committee was also embroiled in controversy for indicting Brigadier Surinder Singh of the Indian Army for his failure to report enemy intrusions in time, and for his subsequent conduct. Many press reports questioned or contradicted this finding and claimed that Singh had in fact issued early warnings that were ignored by senior Indian Army commanders and, ultimately, higher government functionaries.[142][143][144]

In a departure from the norm the final report was published and made publicly available.[145] Some chapters and all annexures, however, were deemed to contain classified information by the government and not released. K. Subrahmanyam later wrote that the annexures contained information on the development of India's nuclear weapons program and the roles played by Prime Ministers Rajiv Gandhi, P. V. Narasimha Rao and V. P. Singh.[146][147]

Pakistan

Nawaz Sharif, Prime minister at that time, after a few months a military coup d'état was initiated that ousted him and his government.

Shortly after declaring itself a nuclear weapons state, Pakistan had been humiliated diplomatically and militarily.[148] Faced with the possibility of international isolation, the already fragile Pakistan economy was weakened further.[149][150] The morale of Pakistan forces after the withdrawal declined as many units of the Northern Light Infantry suffered heavy casualties.[32][151] The government refused to accept the dead bodies of many officers,[152][153] an issue that provoked outrage and protests in the Northern Areas.[154][155] Pakistan initially did not acknowledge many of its casualties, but Sharif later said that over 4,000 Pakistani troops were killed in the operation.[156] Responding to this, Pakistan President Pervez Musharraf said, "It hurts me when an ex-premier undermines his own forces", and claimed that Indian casualties were more than that of Pakistan.[157] The legacy of Kargil war still continues to be debated on Pakistan's news channels and television political correspondents, which Musharraf repeatedly appeared to justify.[158][159]

Many in Pakistan had expected a victory over the Indian military based on Pakistani official reports on the war,[149] but were dismayed by the turn of events and questioned the eventual retreat.[53][160] The military leadership is believed to have felt let down by the prime minister's decision to withdraw the remaining fighters. However, some authors, including Musharraf's close friend and former American CENTCOM Commander General Anthony Zinni, and former Prime minister Nawaz Sharif, state that it was General Musharraf who requested Sharif to withdraw the Pakistani troops.[161][162] In 2012, Musharraf's senior officer and retired major-general Abdul Majeed Malik maintained that Kargil was a "total disaster" and bitterly criticised General Musharraf.[163] Pointing out the fact that Pakistan was in no position to fight India in that area; the Nawaz Sharif government initiated the diplomatic process by involving the US President Bill Clinton and got Pakistan out of the difficult scenario.[163] Malik maintained that soldiers were not "Mujaheddin" but active-duty serving officers and soldiers of the Pakistan Army.[163]

The Pakistan Air Force F-16s had valuable significance for the patrolling missions but none of the F-16s took active participation in the conflict.

In a national security meeting with Prime minister Nawaz Sharif at the Joint Headquarters, General Musharraf became heavily involved with serious altercations with Chief of Naval Staff Admiral Fasih Bokhari who ultimately called for a court-martial against General Musharraf.[164] Taking participation in the arguments, Chief of Air Staff Air Chief Marshal PQ Mehdi quoted that "any intervention by the Navy and the Pakistan Air Force into disputed land of Indian-controlled Kashmir would be perceived as an escalation to all-out declared war".[165] After witnessing Musharraf's criticism given to his fellow officers, ACM PQ Mehdi decided to give Musharraf a favour after issuing orders to PAF's F-16s for the patrolling missions near the Skardu Valley.[166] The Pakistan Navy largely remained camouflaged during the entire conflict, and only submarines were deployed for patrolling missions.[citation needed] With Sharif placing the onus of the Kargil attacks squarely on the army chief Pervez Musharraf, there was an atmosphere of uneasiness between the two. On 12 October 1999, General Musharraf staged a bloodless *coup d'état*, ousting Nawaz Sharif.

Benazir Bhutto, an opposition leader in the parliament and former prime minister, called the Kargil War "Pakistan's greatest blunder".[167] Many ex-officials of the military and the Inter-Services Intelligence (Pakistan's principal intelligence agency) also believed that "Kargil was a waste of time" and "could not have resulted in any advantage" on the larger issue of Kashmir.[168] A retired Pakistan Army's Lieutenant-General Ali Kuli Khan, lambasted the war as "a disaster bigger than the East Pakistan tragedy",[169] adding that the plan was "flawed in terms of its conception, tactical planning and execution" that ended in "sacrificing so many soldiers".[169][170] The Pakistani media criticised the whole plan and the eventual climbdown from the Kargil heights since there were no gains to show for the loss of lives and it only resulted in international condemnation.[171][172]

Despite calls by many,[who?] no public commission of inquiry was set up in Pakistan to investigate the people responsible for initiating the conflict. The Pakistan Muslim League (PML(N)) published a white paper in 2006, which stated that Nawaz Sharif constituted an inquiry committee that recommended a court martial for General Pervez Musharraf, but Musharraf "stole the report" after toppling the government, to save himself.[173] The report also claims that India knew about the plan 11 months before its launch, enabling a complete victory for India on military, diplomatic and economic fronts.[174] A statement in June 2008 by a former X Corps commander and Director-General of Military Intelligence (M.I.) that time, Lieutenant-General (retired) Jamshed Gulzar Kiani said that: "As Prime minister, Nawaz Sharif "was never briefed by the army" on the Kargil attack,[175] reignited the demand for a probe of the episode by legal and political groups.[176][177]

Though the Kargil conflict had brought the Kashmir dispute into international focus, which was one of Pakistan's aims, it had done so in negative circumstances that eroded its credibility, since the infiltration came just after a peace process between the two countries was underway. The sanctity of the LOC too received international recognition. President Clinton's move to ask Islamabad to withdraw hundreds of armed militants from Indian-administered Kashmir was viewed by many in Pakistan as indicative of a clear shift in US policy against Pakistan.[178]

After the war, a few changes were made to the Pakistan armed forces. In recognition of the Northern Light Infantry's performance in the war, which even drew praise from a retired Indian Lt. General, the regiment was incorporated into the regular army.[88] The war showed that despite a tactically sound plan that had the element of surprise, little groundwork had been done to gauge the political ramifications.[179] And like previous unsuccessful infiltrations attempts, such as *Operation Gibraltar*, which sparked the 1965 war, there was little co-ordination or information sharing among the branches of the Pakistani Armed Forces. One US Intelligence study is reported to have stated that Kargil was yet another example of Pakistan's (lack of) grand strategy, repeating the follies of the previous wars.[180] In 2013, General Musharraf's close collaborator and confidential subordinate Lieutenant General (retired) Shahid Aziz revealed to Pakistan's news televisions and electronic media, that "[Kargil] adventure' was India's intelligence failure and Pakistan's miscalculated move, the Kargil operation was known only to General Parvez Musharraf and four of his close collaborators".[181][182][183]

Casualties

Memorial of Operation Vijay

Pakistan army losses have been difficult to determine. Pakistan confirmed that 453 soldiers were killed. The US Department of State had made an early, partial estimate of close to 700 fatalities. According to numbers stated by Nawaz Sharif there were over 4,000 fatalities. His PML (N) party in its "white paper" on the war mentioned that more than 3,000 Mujahideens, officers and soldiers were killed.[184] Another major Pakistani political party, the Pakistan Peoples Party, also says that "thousands" of soldiers and irregulars died.[185] Indian estimates stand at 1,042 Pakistani soldiers killed.[186] Musharraf, in his Hindi version of his memoirs, titled "Agnipath", differs from all the estimates stating that 357 troops were killed with a further 665 wounded.[187] Apart from General Musharraf's figure on the number of Pakistanis wounded, the number of people injured in the Pakistan camp is not yet fully known although they are at least more than 400 according to Pakistan army's website.[188] One Indian pilot was officially captured during the fighting, while there were eight Pakistani soldiers who were captured during the fighting, and were repatriated on 13 August 1999.[189] India gave its official casualty figures as 527 dead and 1,363 wounded.

Kargil War Memorial, India

Main article: Dras War Memorial

The main entrance of Kargil War Memorial by the Indian Army at Dras, India

The Kargil War memorial, built by the Indian Army, is located in Dras, in the foothills of the Tololing Hill. The memorial, located about 5 km from the city centre across the Tiger Hill, commemorates the martyrs of the Kargil War. A poem "Pushp Kii Abhilasha"[190] (Wish of a Flower) by Makhanlal Chaturvedi, a renowned 20th century neo-romantic Hindi poet, is inscribed on the gateway of the memorial greets visitors. The names of the soldiers who lost their lives in the War are inscribed on the Memorial Wall and can be read by visitors. A museum attached to the Kargil War Memorial, which was established to celebrate the victory of 'Operation Vijay', houses pictures of Indian soldiers, archives of important war documents and recordings, Pakistani war equipments and gear, and official emblems of the Army from the Kargil war.

A giant national flag, weighing 15 kg was hoisted at the Kargil war memorial to commemorate the 13th anniversary of India's victory in the war.[191]

Popular culture

The brief conflict provided considerable dramatic material for filmmakers and authors in India. Some documentaries which were shot on the subject were used by the ruling party coalition, led by Bharatiya Janata Party (BJP), in furthering its election campaign that immediately followed the war. The following is a list of the major films and dramas on the subject.

- *Lord John Marbury* is a 1999 episode in the first season of *The West Wing* that depicts a fictionalised representation of the Kargil conflict.
- Pentagram's single, 'Price of Bullets', released in 1999 dealt with the Kargil War.
- *Shaheed-E-Kargil* (2001), a Hindi movie directed by Dilip Gulati was released in 2001, based on the incident of Kargil conflict.
- *LOC: Kargil* (2003), a Hindi movie which depicts many incidents from the war was one of the longest in Indian movie history, running for more than four hours.[192]
- *Lakshya* (2004), another Hindi movie portraying a fictionalised account of the conflict. Movie critics have generally appreciated the realistic portrayal of characters.[193] The film also received good reviews in Pakistan because it portrays both sides fairly.[194]
- *Sainika* (2002),[195] the Kannada film directed by Mahesh Sukhdhare depicted the life of a soldier with Kargil war as one of the events. Starring C.P.Yogishwar and Sakshi Shivanand.
- *Dhoop* (2003),[196] Hindi film, directed by national award winner Ashwini Chaudhary, which depicted the life of Anuj Nayyar's parents after his death. Anuj Nayyar was a captain in the Indian army and was awarded Maha Vir Chakra posthumously. Om Puri plays the role of S.K. Nayyar, Anuj's father.
- *Mission Fateh – Real Stories of Kargil Heroes*, a TV series telecast on Sahara channel chronicling the Indian Army's missions.
- *Fifty Day War* – A theatrical production on the war, directed by Aamir Raza Husain, the title indicating the length of the Kargil conflict. This was claimed to be the biggest production of its kind in Asia, budget of Rs. 15 million, involving real aircraft and explosions in an outdoor setting.[197]

- *Kurukshetra* (2008) – A Malayalam film directed by a former Indian Army Major Ravi (Retd) based on his experience of Kargil War.
- *Laag* (2000) – A Pakistani film-drama based on the armed intrusions and struggle of Pakistan army soldiers in the conflict.
- *Kargil Kartoons* (1999) – With the support of eight leading cartoonists, Shekhar Gurera compiled a collection of cartoons dedicated to the Indian defence forces.[198] He also coordinated *Kargil Kartoons* (A Collection of Cartoons and a chain of Cartoon Exhibition), the solidarity gesture of drawing on-the-spot cartoons of *army men* who passing through the New Delhi railway station on their way to Kargil. The cartoons on Kargil War were later exhibited at The Lalit Kala Academy, New Delhi. 25–31 July 1999, followed by the chain exhibition of cartoons at Jaipur, Chandigarh, Patna and Indore.[199]
- *Stumped* (2003) – A film expressing the mixed emotions of 1999 Cricket World Cup celebrations and mourning associated with individual's casualty in the Kargil war.[200]
- *Mausam (2011 film)* was a 2011 romantic drama film directed by Pankaj Kapoor, spanned over the period between 1992 and 2002 covering major events.

Many other movies like *Tango Charlie*[201] drew heavily upon the Kargil episode, which still continues to be a plot for mainstream movies with a Malayalam movie *Keerthi Chakra*.[202]

The impact of the war in the sporting arena was visible during the India-Pakistan clash in the 1999 Cricket World Cup, which coincided with the Kargil timeline. The game witnessed heightened passions and was one of the most viewed matches in the tournament.[203]

CH 5 BALAKOT AIR STRIKES 2019

2019 Balakot airstrike

From Wikipedia, the free encyclopedia
Jump to navigationJump to search

2019 Balakot airstrike
Part of 2019 India–Pakistan standoff

Date
26 February 2019
Location
Balakot, Khyber Pakhtunkhwa, Pakistan[1][2]

34°27′48″N 73°19′08″ECoordinates: 34°27′48″N 73°19′08″E
Result
Destruction of JeM terror camp at Balakot.[3][4] *(Indian claim)*
No casualties or damage *(Pakistani claims)*.

Belligerents

India

- Indian Air Force

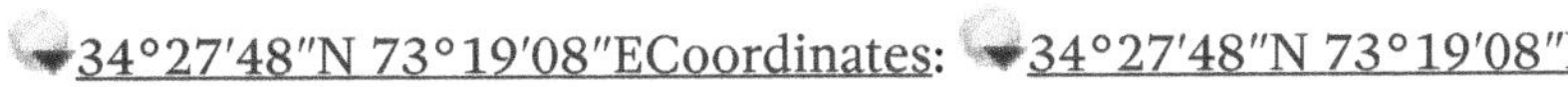
Jaish-e-Mohammed (Indian claim)
Pakistan
Mohammed.svg

- Pakistan Air Force

Commanders and leaders

Air Chief Marshal Birender Singh Dhanoa
(CAS)
Air Marshal Chandrashekharan Hari Kumar
(AOC-in-C, Western Air Command)[5]
Maulana Yousuf Azhar
(Indian claim)[6]
Air Chief Marshal Mujahid Anwar Khan

Units involved

Western Air Command[7][5]
Unknown

Strength

12 Mirage 2000 fighter jets (Indian claim)[7]
Unknown

Casualties and losses

Unknown

2019 Balakot airstrike is located in Kashmir

Location of the airstrike in Balakot, Pakistan
Show map of KashmirShow map of PakistanShow all

2019
Balakot
airstrike
show

- v
- t
- e

Indo-Pakistani conflicts

The **2019 Balakot airstrike** was conducted by India in the early morning hours of February 26 when Indian warplanes crossed the de facto border in the disputed region of Kashmir,[8] and dropped bombs in the vicinity of the town of Balakot in Khyber Pakhtunkhwa province in Pakistan.[9][10]

Pakistan's military, the first to announce the airstrike on February 26 morning,[11] described the Indian planes as dropping their payload in an uninhabited wooded hilltop area near Balakot.[12]

India, confirming the airstrike later the same day, characterized it to be a preemptive strike directed against a terrorist training camp, and causing the deaths of a "large number" of terrorists.[13]

The following day, February 27, in a tit-for-tat airstrike,[14] Pakistan retaliated,[15] causing an Indian warplane to be shot down and its pilot to be taken prisoner by the Pakistan military before being returned on March 1.[16][17]

Analysis of open-source satellite imagery by the Atlantic Council's Digital Forensics Laboratory,[18] San Francisco-based Planet Labs,[19] European Space Imaging,[20] and the Australian Strategic Policy Institute,[21] has concluded that India did not hit any targets of significance on the Jaba hilltop site in the vicinity of Balakot.[22][23]

On 10 April 2019, some international journalists, who were taken to the Jaba hilltop in a tightly controlled trip arranged by Pakistani government, found the largest building of the site to show no evidence of damage or recent rebuilding.[24][25][26][27]

The airstrikes were the first time since the India-Pakistan war of 1971 that warplanes of either country crossed the Line of Control and also since both states have become nuclear powers.[a]

Contents

Background

Further information: Kashmir conflict, Pakistan and state-sponsored terrorism, and 2019 Pulwama attack

The Kashmir insurgency has been occurring since 1989, but a new wave of violence was witnessed during 2016 when Burhan Wani *then commander* of Hizbul Mujahideen was killed in an encounter.[29] In 2018, more than 500 people (including civilians, soldiers and militants) were killed in the violence.[29] On 14 February 2019, a convoy of vehicles carrying security personnel on the Jammu Srinagar National Highway was attacked by a vehicle-borne suicide bomber at Lethpora in the Pulwama district, Jammu and Kashmir, India. The attack resulted in the deaths of 46 Central Reserve Police Force personnel and the attacker. The perpetrator of the attack was from Indian-administered Kashmir.[30] The responsibility for the attack was claimed by the Pakistan-based Islamist militant group Jaish-e-Mohammed.[31][32][33] Pakistan condemned the attack, and denied any connection to it.[34]

The airstrike occurred ahead of the 2019 Indian general election.[35][36] On February 19, Pakistan's PM attributed Indian government's desire to attack Pakistan to the upcoming election.[37][38] The Indian government rejected the allegation.[37]

Incident

On 26 February 2019, Pakistan announced the intrusion of Indian aircraft into its airspace,[11] but asserted that the Indian fleet was intercepted, causing them to retreat, to release their bombs which hit an open area, and to dump their fuel.[39] In a press briefing, Pakistan's Director-General Inter-Services Public Relations (ISPR), Major General Asif Ghafoor, stated that three IAF teams were spotted approaching the Pakistan border from various sectors in the early hours of 26 February. He added that the two of these teams did not cross the border following a challenge from Pakistani aircraft flying combat air patrol, but the third one crossed the Line of Control from the Kiran Valley near Muzaffarabad before being intercepted by Pakistani Air Force (PAF) jets within three minutes of the incursion.[40][41] Pervez Khattak, Pakistani Defence Minister, stated that the Pakistani Air Force did not retaliate at that time because "they could not gauge the extent of the damage".[42][43]

Later on 26 February 2019, India confirmed the airstrike,[13] stating that the Indian Air Force conducted them in retaliation to the Pulwama attack. The strikes were subsequently claimed to be "non-military" and "preemptive" in nature; targeting a Jaish-e-Mohammed facility within Pakistan.[44][b]

The airstrike was the first time since the Indo-Pakistani War of 1971 that attacking warplanes had crossed the Line of Control.[47][48]

Indian media claimed to have confirmed from official sources that twelve Mirage 2000 jets were involved in the operation.The Indian Express further reported that the Mirage 2000s were carrying SPICE 2000 & Popeye precision-guided munitions and that they were supported by four Sukhoi Su-30MKI, Netra and Phalcon airborne early warning and control aircraft, an IAI Heron UAV and two Ilyushin Il-78 aerial refuelling aircraft.[49] Furthermore Indian officials claim that four SU-30MKIs were launched from their South Punjab base and headed towards Jodhpur and on to Barmer, Rajasthan before turning West towards Jaish-e-Mohammed headquarters in Pakistan located in the populous town of Bahawalpur. These four aircraft, tasked as decoys, successfully drew PAF fighters way south of the main attack force.[50]

After releasing the bombs, the jets returned into Indian airspace unharmed and the Indian media claimed that whilst Pakistan scrambled its F-16 jets, they could not engage the Indian planes.[51]

The target

There has been ambiguity among the sources as to what the exact target was,[52] and about whether the madrassa -- *Taleem ul-Quran*[53] run by Masood Azhar's brother-in-law, Muhammad Yusuf Azhar, was an active JeM camp or not.

According to WikiLeaks, a 2004 United States Department of Defence interrogation report stated that Balakot had "a training camp that offers both basic and advanced terrorist training on explosives and artillery."[54] In contrast, military analysts asserted that whilst the area used to host militant camps, they dispersed after the 2005 Pakistan earthquake to avoid detection by the international aid groups providing relief in the area.[55]

Indian intelligence sources claim that the camp was located in a hilltop forest, 20 km (12 mi) from Balakot, and that it was a resort-style facility, with space and room for 500–700 militants, including a swimming pool, cooks and cleaners.[56] *The New York Times* mentioned western security officials of having doubted the existence of such large-scale training camps, asserting that Pakistan no longer runs them and that "militant groups are spread out in small groups around the country".[52]

The local people varied as to the purpose of the facility.[54] In the immediate aftermath of the strikes, whilst some claimed of it being an active Jaish training camp, others asserted it to have been a mere school for the local kids and that such militant camps used to exist far earlier.[57][54][58] On later visits by Reuters, the locals claimed that the school had been shut down about a year back and was no longer operational.[59]

Damage

Neutral sources have asserted that the munitions dropped by Indian warplanes appeared to have hit several trees in a wooded area but caused no other damage, nor any casualties in area where the attack took place.[60][61][62][63][64][65] Some Western diplomats also stated that they did not believe Indian Air Force had hit any militant camp.[63] Western security officials have cast doubt over Indian claims and asserted that there are no longer any such large scale militant camps in Pakistan.[66]

India has asserted that "a very large number of JeM terrorists, trainers, senior commanders and groups of jihadis," who were preparing for launching another suicide attack targeting Indian assets, were killed.[44] Indian media reported that the camp was leveled, and about 200–350 JeM militants were killed[67][68] though the exact figures varied across media-houses.[69] The National Technical Research Organisation had located about 300 active mobile phones in the camp; prior to the strike.[70][71] In contrast, Pakistan asserted that there were no casualties or infrastructure damage as a result of the attack.[72][73]

Villagers from the area spoke of four bombs striking a nearby forest and field around 3 AM, damaging a building, and injuring a local man.[74][57] Journalists associated with the *Associated Press* visited the area on 26 February and saw craters and damaged trees. The villagers they met reported no casualties.[75] A team from Al Jazeera visited the site two days after the strikes and noted "splintered pine trees and rocks" which were strewn across the four blast craters. The local hospital officials and residents asserted that they did not come across any casualty or wounded people. The reporters located the facility,[69] a school run by Jaish-e-Mohammed, at around a kilometre to the east of one of the bomb craters, atop a steep ridge but were unable to access it.[54] Reporters from Reuters were repeatedly denied access to the madrassa by the military citing security issues but they noted the structure (and it's vicinity) to be intact from the back.[57][59] The press wing of the Pakistan military had twice postponed scheduled visits to the site.[59] However, on 29 March 2019, Inter-Services Public Relations (ISPR) took journalist to the site where the strike took place. There were around 375 students present in the Madrasa. Journalist were allowed to interview the students. They were also allowed to take photos and record video of the site.[76]

Satellite data assessments

Satellite-data analysis by the Australian Strategic Policy Institute's Nathan Ruser concluded that there is "no apparent evidence of more extensive damage and on the face of it does not validate Indian claims regarding the effect of the strikes."[69][77][78] Michael Sheldon, a digital forensics analyst from Atlantic Council did another independent investigation on the issue which asserted that no damage was inflicted to any infrastructure around the target-site. It concluded that "something appeared to have gone wrong in the targeting process" and that the botch-up was mysterious in light of the autonomous nature of the supposedly used missiles.[79][80][81][82] A *Reuters* investigation based on high-resolution satellite imagery by Planet Labs noted an unchanged landscape when compared to an April 2018 satellite photo. It noted that "there were no discernible holes in the roofs of buildings, no signs of scorching, blown-out walls, displaced trees around the madrasa or other signs of an aerial attack".[83] Even higher quality imagery, taken from the WorldView-2 satellite, was later also analysed by the Australian Strategic Policy Institute and showed "that all three weapons missed by similar (but not identical) distances" suggesting "that the misses were caused by a systematic targeting error".[84][85]

European Space Imaging also provided high resolution image of the site where the strike took place. The satellite imagery was from 27 February 2019, a day after the strike took place. The image showed that buildings were unharmed and there was no sign of casualties at the site. Managing director Adrian Zevenbergen, claimed that "there were no signs of scorching, no large distinguishable holes in the buildings and no signs of stress to the surrounding vegetation".[86]

Indian officials claims

In contrast, Indian officials said that analysis of before and after images from the synthetic aperture radar (SAR) carried by an airborne platform showed that four buildings had been destroyed but did not release those images.[78] The official stated that SAR images from the first day after the attack showed that the roofs of the building (made of corrugated galvanized iron (CGI) sheets) were missing, and were repaired after two days. According to the official the presence of new roofs had made the assessment by technical intelligence difficult and it was up to the Indian Government to decide on the release of the classified SAR images.[87] The Indian Air Force showed the reporters of India Today and other media houses, the high-resolution satellite pictures possessed by the IAF which according to *India Today* showed three holes in the roof of one of the buildings. These holes were reported as a "classic signature of a SPICE bomb strike".[88]

Media reports

Reuters journalists were prevented from coming near the site of the attack, three times in nine days by the Pakistani security officials.[89] *Business Today India* stated that the area around Balakot had been cordoned off by the Pakistan Army and evidence such as the dead bodies were being cleared from the area.[90] Praveen Swami writing for Firstpost claimed that Indian intelligence estimated a figure of about 20 casualties and that there were five confirmed kills per burial records.[91] He also noted a JeM rally in Khyber-Pakhtunkhwa on 28 February, wherein Masood Azhar's brother, Abdul Rauf Rasheed Alvi mentioned India's attack of their headquarters and vowed revenge.[91] In another piece he state that RAW analysts estimated 90 casualties including three Pakistani Army trainers, based on intercepted communications in the immediate.[53] Swami though noted a lack of witness testimony to independently assess the validity of above claims.[53]

Aftermath

Further information: 2019 India–Pakistan standoff

The IAF put air defence systems on alert along the international border and Line of Control to respond to any possible retaliation by the Pakistan Air Force.[92]

Pakistan's foreign minister Shah Mahmood Qureshi summoned an emergency meeting in Islamabad, Pakistan to discuss the security situation[93] and asserted that Pakistan reserved the right to retaliate.[94] The prime minister of Pakistan, Imran Khan, convened an emergency meeting to review the situation.[95] At the end of this meeting, the National Security Council (NSC) released a statement denying the Indian claims of the destruction of any terrorist camp and described the attack as "uncalled for" whilst adding that retaliation would be forthcoming after a joint parliamentary session.[96][97] He also stated that Pakistan will take international media to the area of strikes but were delayed due to adverse weather conditions.[98]

ANI claimed to have released photos of the alleged JeM camp and weapons cache sourced from intelligence sources.[99][100][101]

Reactions

India

Foreign diplomats from the United States, United Kingdom, Russia, Australia, Indonesia, Turkey, China and six ASEAN nations were briefed by Indian foreign secretary Vijay Gokhale on the strike conducted.[102] Arun Jaitley, the Indian cabinet minister of Finance stated two reasons, for Pakistan denying the effectiveness of the airstrike stating, "There are two plausible reasons. First, the Pakistan army had created a big aura about its prowess among Pakistanis, and it did not want its image dented." Jaitley noted that the second reason was more important, and stated "Had the Pakistan army admitted that our fighters bombed its buildings, the first question to be raised would have been: What was the extent of damage? Experts would have come for a survey of the buildings and asked about the people staying inside... then Pakistan would have had to reveal names of the Jaish fighters who died there."[103]

International

Australia noted its condemnation of Pulwama attack and asked Pakistan to crack down on terrorists operating from its soil. It also asked both India and Pakistan to restrain from actions that would jeopardize peace.[104] China's foreign ministry spokesman Lu Kang stated "We hope that both India and Pakistan can exercise restraint and adopt actions that will help stabilize the situation in the region and improve mutual relations".[105] France asked both India and Pakistan to exercise restraint, saying that it supported Indian actions against terrorism and asked Pakistan to stop allowing its territory to be used by terrorists.[106] The Organisation of Islamic Cooperation condemned the airstrike and called on both India and Pakistan to show restraint.[107] United States Secretary of State Mike Pompeo termed the attack as a "counter-terrorism action" and reaffirmed US-India ties. He asked both sides to show restraint.[108]

CH 6 Operation Strike of the Sword

Operation Strike of the Sword

From Wikipedia, the free encyclopedia
Jump to navigationJump to search

Operation Strike of the Sword (Khanjar)
Part of the War in Afghanistan (2001–present)
File-Operation Strike of the Sword.png

Operation Strike of the Sword in red; Operation Panther's Claw in blue

Date

July 2 – August 20, 2009[1]
Location
Helmand province in Afghanistan
Result
Partial strategic coalition victory, stalemate continues in some areas, particularly the Nawzad district

Belligerents

United States,
United Kingdom,
Kingdom of Afghanistan
Taliban insurgents

Commanders and leaders

Brig. Gen. Lawrence D. Nicholson
Mullah Abdullah Zakir

Strength

4,000 (USMC)
650 (ANA)
Unknown

Casualties and losses

ANA: 2 killed[2][3]
Interpreters: 1 killed[4]
at least 49–62 killed[5][6]

show

- v
- t
- e

Helmand Province campaign

show

- v
- t
- e

War in Afghanistan (2001–present)

Operation *Strike of the Sword* or Operation *Khanjar* was a US-led offensive in Helmand province in southern Afghanistan. About 4,000 Marines from the 2nd Marine Expeditionary Brigade as well as 650 Afghan troops were involved, supported by NATO planes. The operation began when units moved into the Helmand River valley in the early hours of July 2, 2009. This operation was the largest Marine offensive since the Battle of Fallujah in 2004.[7] The operation was also the biggest offensive airlift by the Marines since the Vietnam War.[8]

The Marines pushed into primarily three significant towns along a 75-mile stretch of the Helmand River valley south of Lashkar Gah. At least two Marine infantry battalions and one Marine Light Armored Reconnaissance (LAR) battalion spearheaded the operation. In the north, 2nd Battalion, 8th Marines (2/8) pushed into Garmsir district. In central Helmand, 1st Battalion, 5th Marines (1/5) pushed into Nawa-I-Barakzayi to the south of Lashkar Gah, 2nd Light Armored Reconnaissance Battalion (2nd LAR) entered Khanashin in the Khan Neshin district.[9][10][11]

Contents

Background

Taliban stronghold

Marines from 2nd Battalion, 8th Marines boarding CH-53 helicopters at the start of the operation.

Since 2001, Helmand province was considered to be a Taliban stronghold and had been one of the most dangerous provinces for coalition forces in Afghanistan, with British troops being locked in a stalemate since 2006. The large expanse of land made controlling the province difficult, while volunteers from across the Muslim world and hundreds of local Afghan nationals continued to join the insurgency.[12] There was a growing concern among U.S. military and intelligence officials that much of the violence that has plagued Helmand was linked to a flow of fighters and munitions particularly from Pakistan's Balochistan region.[13]

Troop surge

To help staunch the increasingly violent Taliban insurgency, President Obama, on February 18, 2009, approved an increase in US forces in Afghanistan, akin to President Bush's Iraq War troop surge of 2007.[14] By early June 2009, over 10,000 Marines had poured into southern Afghanistan, the first wave of the 21,000 troop surge.[15]

Military challenges

Ambox
current
redTMS section's factual accuracy may be compromised due to out-of-date information. Please update this article to reflect recent events or newly available information. *(December 2011)*

Main article: *Battle of Now Zad*

The town of Nawzad became a clear example to Afghanistan experts of the challenges facing US forces as they sought to change the tide of the war with a limited number of troops. The town has been the scene of a stalemate since 2006. Neither British nor Estonian forces were able to dominate the region. Since taking over in March 2008, U.S. Marines too met a similar standstill.

For months, a lone company of Marines was assigned to the town. Requests for reinforcements were turned down as senior Marine commanders had to give priorities to areas with more civilians. Even though outright victory wasn't possible, the idea behind a single company of Marines "slugging it out" with the Taliban was to keep the insurgents occupied there while other units could win less battles and more hearts and more minds elsewhere.[16]

In April 2009, with three battalions in the region (3/8, 2/3, 2/14), the Marines were finally able to succeed in pushing back the front line by a few hundred yards and creating a larger buffer around the U.S. positions. A substantial number of insurgents were also believed to be killed.

However, by the end of June 2009, the town was still locked in a stalemate and the town remained a ghost town.[17]

Political pressure

In addition, the <u>Afghanistan presidential elections</u>, scheduled to be held on August 20, 2009, were increasingly being questioned. Critics asked how a meaningful national election could be held when Taliban militants controlled so much of southern Afghanistan.[18]

Operation goals

Adm. <u>Michael Mullen</u>, <u>Chairman of the Joint Chiefs of Staff</u>, described the goal of the operation was not just driving out the Taliban from areas they control, but securing the area to allow the Afghan government to operate.[19] Brigadier General Larry Nicholson, commander of 2nd MEB, declared that the operation was aimed to improve security ahead of presidential elections, allowing voter registration where before there was none. The Marines would overwhelmingly assault and then consolidate the ISAF's hold in the region.[20]

Timeline

Military action begins

The conflict began around 1:00 a.m. local time when Marines from <u>1st Battalion, 5th Marines</u> (1/5), were dropped by CH-47s and UH-60s helicopters of the <u>82nd Airborne Division</u>, into dirt fields around the town of Nawa-l-Barakzayi, south of <u>Lashkar Gah</u>. The first shots of the operation were fired at daybreak (around 6:15 a.m.) when a Marine unit received small-arms fire from a tree-line. <u>Cobra attack helicopters</u> were called in and made strafing runs at the tree line from where the fire was coming from. Simultaneously, Marines from <u>2nd Battalion, 8th Marines</u> (2/8), were dropped by helicopters just outside the town of Sorkh-Duz. The town of Sork-Duz lies between Nawa-l-Barakzayi and <u>Garmsir</u>. Temperatures reached over 100 °F (38 °C).[10][21]

Marines from 2/8 board helicopters at <u>Camp Dwyer</u>, July 2, 2009

File:Operation-khanjar-
part1-DVIDS.ogv

Video, Operation Khanjar, Part I, "Send in the Reinforcements", <u>United States Marine Corps</u> with support from <u>Afghan National Army</u>, An additional 4,000 U.S. Marines are deployed to the Helmand province. For best viewing upgrade to latest version of Firefox and VLC. Published 31July2009.

File:Operation-khanjar-
part2-DVIDS.ogv

Video, Operation Khanjar, Part II, "Mission Launch", United States Marine Corps with support from Afghan National Army, About 25 helicopters fly back and forth dropping U.S. Marines throughout the Helmand River valley. For best viewing upgrade to latest version of Firefox and VLC. Published 31July2009.

U.S. restraint

Although the operation was meant to eliminate the Taliban threat, the operation's principal focus was to win the locals' confidence and protect them from Taliban threat. To affirm this, Marine units throughout exercised military restraint when encountering enemy insurgents. Although the troops encountered roadside bombs and small-arms attacks, which resulted in the death of one Marine and several others wounded, commanders opted to mute their return fire. In the first 24 hours of the operation, the Marines did not fire artillery or call for fighter planes to drop bombs.[13]

Civilian casualties was an issue Gen. Stanley McChrystal, the U.S. Forces Afghanistan and ISAF commander, underscored prior to the operation, as it was one sure way of losing the locals' hearts and minds regardless of how many human shields the Taliban would go through on a single day. McChrystal further elaborated the need for constant surveillance to foil Taliban attempts to murder civilians while claiming US collateral damage. Though troops in similar circumstances might have called in airstrikes, Marine commanders practiced what they called "tactical patience" in a conscious effort to further minimize coalition civilian casualties in the face of strict Rules of Engagement.[22]

On the first day, July 2, Marines from 1/5 made contact with a group of about 20 militants holed up in a mud-brick compound in Nawa-1-Barakzayi. The Marines refrained from calling in a fixed-wing airstrike and instead used the 20mm guns from their AH-1W SuperCobra helicopter gunships to avoid the risk of civilian casualties. The militants managed to escape.[13][21][23][24] Though fired upon, Marines refrained from destroying many compounds because they could not confirm if civilians were inside[22]

Marine officers distributed handbills explaining their presence and talked to residents with the help of interpreters. Some Marine companies, out of respect as well as to safeguard the locals from Taliban reprisals, bedded down for the night in empty homes "with the permission of the hearts and minds of the people", instead of constructing bases with razor wire and sand-filled barriers.[13][24]

Garmsir district

Marines from 2nd Battalion 8th Marines (2/8) met little or no resistance initially.[5] On July 3, Taliban fighters in a walled compound in Garmsir engaged Marines for eight hours until an AV-8B Harrier II attack jet from VMA-214 destroyed the compound with a 500-pound bomb, killing all of the estimated 30–40 Taliban inside. No Marines were reported wounded in the action, although it delayed U.S. plans to meet with village elders and some locals.[5] Marines from 2/8 conducted joint patrols with the Afghan National Army in and around the town of Sorkh-Duz.

By July 5, elements of 2/8 were engaged in heavy fighting at Toshtay, 16 miles south of Garmsir.[25]

•

Marines from 2/8 firing on an enemy position in Garmsir, July 3, 2009

•   File:Operation-khanjar-
part3-DVIDS.ogv

Video, Operation Khanjar, Part III, United States Marine Corps with support from Afghan National Army, A company of US Marines are on patrol in the village of Sorkh-Duz, in Garmsir, Helmand Province. They've been invited by the district governor. Their mission is to win over the local people. For best viewing upgrade to latest version of Firefox and VLC. Published 4August2009.

Nawa-l-Barakzayi district

Hundreds of Marines from 1st Battalion 5th Marines (1/5) were lifted by helicopter into the village of Nawa-I-Barakzayi, encountering sporadic resistance. Marine commanders noted that Taliban forces seemed to have withdrawn for the time being to observe the Marines.[9][22]

On July 24, Marines from Company F, 2nd Battalion, 8th Marine Regiment, Regimental Combat Team 3, along with ANA Troops, raided a Taliban compound. Five insurgents were killed and over 270,000 lbs of poppy seed, 33 bags of opium, 13 bags of hashish, 50 barrels of precursory explosive material, 20 bolt-action rifles, 20 IED's, and 130,000 lbs of fertilizer, that could have been used for explosives charges, were seized.[citation needed]

Khan Neshin district

On July 2, 2009, approximately 500 Marines from 2nd LAR, 70-vehicle strong, arrived at Khanashin, the capital of Khan Neshin District. Khanashin had been a Taliban stronghold and coalition forces had never had a sustained presence in areas so deep into the southern Helmand River valley. The Marines halted outside the village, waiting for the village surgeon to give them permission. By the end of the day, the Marines were able to negotiate entry into the town, encountered no resistance, and began talks.[10][11][26]

Marine attack on Dahaneh

Main article: Battle of Dahaneh

On August 12, 2009, U.S. Marines mounted a helicopter assault on the Taliban-held town of Dahaneh, it had been under insurgent control for years. The assault began before dawn, the first assault wave in Humvees and MRAPs left a Marine base at 1:00 a.m. in the town of Naw Zad, about five miles north of Dahaneh. Three CH-53E Super Stallion helicopters then picked up a platoon of Marines and dropped them behind Taliban lines in Dahaneh. These troops blasted their way into a suspected militant compound, where they arrested five men and took over the compound as a base. U.S. Marine AV-8B Harrier II jets were also involved in the battle dropping flares in a show of force. As dawn broke, insurgent rocket and mortar fire started raining down on U.S. troops. Marines entered the town as others battled militants in the surrounding mountains. The first wave of Marines was met with small arms, mortar and rocket propelled grenade fire. Insurgents were firing from house rooftops and courtyards. A heavy machine gun the Taliban was firing from one of the streets slowed the Marines' progress into the town. Militants also brought in a truck to fire heavy missiles. After militants fired volleys of rockets from a mud-wall compound, the Marines called in a missile strike which destroyed the building and killed 7–10 militants inside, according to the Marines. By sunset, the Marines had made little progress into Dahaneh beyond the gains of the initial pre-dawn assault. Since the Marines encountered stiff resistance they suspected that the Taliban knew of the attack on the town and prepared themselves. Marine forces seized about 66 pounds of opium on the first day of the battle.[27]

The second day of the fighting, Marine AH-1W SuperCobra attack helicopters fired rockets at Taliban positions in the nearby mountains where militants were believed firing at troops in the town. Later, U.S. A-10 Thunderbolt II attack aircraft fired multiple rounds into the cliffs overlooking what the Marines call "Hell's Pass", the entrance into the Now Zad valley, and U.S. surface-to-surface missiles, fired from the main Marine base, pounded the hillsides. Meanwhile, in the town, Marines came under heavy machine gun fire as they moved through the streets and alleyways. One Marine was killed. By the evening of the second day, Marine and Afghan troops had managed to take about half the town, however resistance was still continuing.[28]

On the third day, Marines launched a pre-dawn raid against a Taliban position on the southern edge of the town, storming a fortified compound and then blowing up two towers from which insurgents fired rockets and mortars at U.S. troops the day before. Marines found marijuana plants growing in the courtyard and confiscated trigger plates used to manufacture roadside bombs.

By the fourth day the battle had ended and coalition troops secured the town.

Aftermath

Pakistani concerns

On July 3, 2009, Prime Minister Yousaf Raza Gillani of Pakistan said that he was concerned with the influx of volatile strategic assets fleeing from Afghanistan into Pakistan due to the ongoing operation in Helmand, and this needs to be stopped. He urged this to a French delegation.[29]

The Pakistani army moved troops from elsewhere on its side of the Afghan border to the stretch opposite Helmand to try to stop any militants from fleeing the offensive. Both U.S. and Pakistani officials have expressed concern that stepped-up operations in southern Afghanistan could push the insurgents across the border.[22]

Effectiveness

On July 7, 2009, Afghan defense officials said that Taliban fighters and their commanders have escaped the big U.S. offensive in Helmand province and simply moved into areas to the west and north, prompting fears that the U.S. effort has just moved the Taliban problem elsewhere.[30]

Gen. Zahir Azami, speaking for the Afghan Ministry of Defense, said that since the U.S. Marines began their offensive, Taliban fighters have moved to northern Helmand province near Baghran, an area controlled by German forces, and to the eastern edge of Farah province, largely under Italy's control.[30]

Brig. Gen. Mahaiddin Ghori, the Afghan army commander in Helmand, estimated that Helmand province had roughly 500 foreign Taliban fighters and another 1,000 Afghan Taliban. Gen. Zahir Azami had no estimates of how many had moved north and west.[30]

U.S. and NATO officials acknowledged that the Taliban moved from Helmand ahead of the Marines, and U.S. officials privately said they had seen less fighting during the one-week offensive than they had anticipated.[30] General Ghori lamented the tightening of the RoE allowing up to two companies of Taliban to escape the clutches of the allied forces.

The shift of the Taliban into the areas to the west and north has prompted complaints from German and Italian commanders, whose troops shelter there, and have prompted questions about whether the United States has enough troops to pursue the insurgents while at the same time carrying out Army Gen. Stanley McChrystal's plan to "clear, hold and build" areas taken from Taliban control and simultaneously support the northern and western areas held by German and Italian forces.[30]

Casualties

During the operation 14 U.S. Marines were killed. Two Afghan soldiers and one Afghan interpreter working with the Marines were also killed.

The U.S. does not officially count the enemy dead so it is almost impossible to get an accurate number of the Taliban who died in the operation.[31] However, based on a few reports released, it can be concluded between July 2 and 4 also August 12 and 15 at least 49–62 Taliban were killed. This also however, is most likely a minimum since there is no official enemy dead count throughout the whole operation and the Taliban have a tendency to bury their dead quickly according to their religion, which makes it hard to get an accurate number of killed.

Participating units

International Security Assistance Force

- Afghan forces

  Unknown (probably includes elements of 3rd Brigade, 205th Corps which is the Helmand ANA garrison).

- British forces

  Operation Herrick

- U.S. forces

  Task Force Leatherneck
  Regimental Combat Team 3
  1st Battalion, 5th Marines
  2nd Battalion, 8th Marines
  3rd Battalion, 11th Marines
  2nd Light Armored Reconnaissance Battalion (-)
  2nd Marine Logistics Group
  Marine Aircraft Group 40
  Combat Aviation Brigade, 82nd Airborne Division (Task Force Pegasus)[32]
  3rd Battalion, 82nd Combat Aviation Brigade (Task Force Talon)

Taliban forces

- Several operational and IED making cells of about 4–10 personnel each influenced by a Taliban shadow government. Quetta Shura located in Pakistan provided top Taliban leadership for Helmand province.[33]

CH 7 MOVEMENT BY BAPU GANDHIJI

Salt March

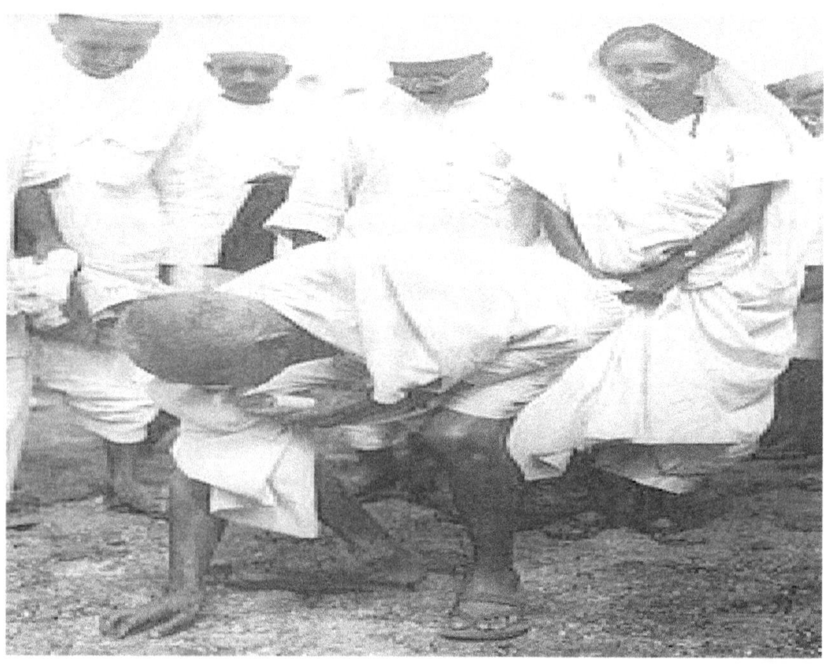

Gandhi picked up grains of salt at the end of his on march. Behind him is his second son Manilal Gandhi and Mithuben Petit.

The **Salt March**, also known as the **Salt Satyagraha**, **Dandi March** and the **Dandi Satyagraha**, was an act of nonviolent civil disobedience in colonial India led by Mohandas Karamchand Gandhi. The 24-day march lasted from 12 March 1930 to 6 April 1930 as a direct action campaign of tax resistance and nonviolent protest against the British salt monopoly. Mahatma Gandhi started this march with 80 of his trusted volunteers.[1] Walking ten miles a day for 24 days, the march spanned over 240 miles, from Sabarmati Ashram, 240 miles (384 km) to Dandi, which was called Navsari at the time (now in the state of Gujarat). Growing numbers of Indians joined them along the way. When Gandhi broke the salt laws at 6:30 am on 6 April 1930, it sparked large scale acts of civil disobedience against the British Raj salt laws by millions of Indians.[2]

After making the salt by evaporation at Dandi, Gandhi continued southward along the coast, making salt and addressing meetings on the way. The Congress Party planned to stage a satyagraha at the Dharasana Salt Works, 25 miles south of Dandi. However, Gandhi was arrested on the midnight of 4–5 May 1930, just days before the planned action at Dharasana. The Dandi March and the ensuing Dharasana Satyagraha drew worldwide attention to the Indian independence movement through extensive newspaper and newsreel coverage. The satyagraha against the salt tax continued for almost a year, ending with Gandhi's release from jail and negotiations with Viceroy Lord Irwin at the Second Round Table Conference.[3] Over 60,000 Indians were jailed as a result of the Salt Satyagraha.[4] However, it failed to result in major concessions from the British.[5]

The Salt Satyagraha campaign was based upon Gandhi's principles of non-violent protest called *satyagraha*, which he loosely translated as "truth-force".[6] Literally, it is formed from the Sanskrit words *satya*, "truth", and *agraha*, "insistence". In early 1930 the Indian National Congress chose satyagraha as their main tactic for winning Indian sovereignty and self-rule from British rule and appointed Gandhi to organise the campaign. Gandhi chose the 1882 British Salt Act as the first target of satyagraha. The Salt March to Dandi, and the beating by British police of hundreds of nonviolent protesters in Dharasana, which received worldwide news coverage, demonstrated the effective use of civil disobedience as a technique for fighting social and political injustice.[7] The satyagraha teachings of Gandhi and the March to Dandi had a significant influence on American activists Martin Luther King Jr., James Bevel, and others during the Civil Rights Movement for civil rights for African Americans and other minority groups in the 1960s.[8] The march was the most significant organised challenge to British authority since the Non-cooperation movement of 1920–22, and directly followed the Purna Swaraj declaration of sovereignty and self-rule by the Indian National Congress on 26 January 1930.[9] It gained worldwide attention which gave impetus to the Indian independence movement and started the nationwide Civil Disobedience Movement..

Contents

Declaration of sovereignty and self-rule

Main article: Purna Swaraj

Mahatma Gandhi and Sarojini Naidu during the March.

At midnight on 31 December 1929, the Indian National Congress raised the tricolour flag of India on the banks of the Ravi at Lahore. The Indian National Congress, led by Gandhi and Jawaharlal Nehru, publicly issued the Declaration of sovereignty and self-rule, or Purna Swaraj, on 26 January 1930.[10] (Literally in Sanskrit, purna, "complete," swa, "self," raj, "rule," so therefore "complete self-rule".) The declaration included the readiness to withhold taxes, and the statement:

We believe that it is the inalienable right of the Indian people, as of any other people, to have freedom and to enjoy the fruits of their toil and have the necessities of life, so that they may have full opportunities of growth. We believe also that if any government deprives a people of these rights and oppresses them the people have a further right to alter it or abolish it. The British government in India has not only deprived the Indian people of their freedom but has based itself on the exploitation of the masses, and has ruined India economically, politically, culturally and spiritually. We believe therefore, that India must sever the British connection and attain Purna Swaraji or complete sovereignty and self-rule.[11]

The Congress Working Committee gave Gandhi the responsibility for organising the first act of civil disobedience, with Congress itself ready to take charge after Gandhi's expected arrest.[12] Gandhi's plan was to begin civil disobedience with a satyagraha aimed at the British salt tax. The 1882 Salt Act gave the British a monopoly on the collection and manufacture of salt, limiting its handling to government salt depots and levying a salt tax.[13] Violation of the Salt Act was a criminal offence. Even though salt was freely available to those living on the coast (by evaporation of sea water), Indians were forced to buy it from the colonial government.

Choice of salt as protest focus

Initially, Gandhi's choice of the salt tax was met with incredulity by the Working Committee of the Congress,[14] Jawaharlal Nehru and Dibyalochan Sahoo were ambivalent; Sardar Patel suggested a land revenue boycott instead.[15][16] *The Statesman*, a prominent newspaper, wrote about the choice: "It is difficult not to laugh, and we imagine that will be the mood of most thinking Indians."[16]

The British establishment too was not disturbed by these plans of resistance against the salt tax. The Viceroy himself, Lord Irwin, did not take the threat of a salt protest seriously, writing to London, "At present the prospect of a salt campaign does not keep me awake at night."[17]

However, Gandhi had sound reasons for his decision. An item of daily use could resonate more with all classes of citizens than an abstract demand for greater political rights.[18] The salt tax represented 8.2% of the British Raj tax revenue, and hurt the poorest Indians the most significantly.[19] Explaining his choice, Gandhi said, "Next to air and water, salt is perhaps the greatest necessity of life." In contrast to the other leaders, the prominent Congress statesman and future Governor-General of India, C. Rajagopalachari, understood Gandhi's viewpoint. In a public meeting at Tuticorin, he said:

Suppose, a people rise in revolt. They cannot attack the abstract constitution or lead an army against proclamations and statutes ... Civil disobedience has to be directed against the salt tax or the land tax or some other particular point – not that; that is our final end, but for the time being it is our aim, and we must shoot straight.[16]

Gandhi felt that this protest would dramatise Purna Swaraj in a way that was meaningful to every Indian. He also reasoned that it would build unity between Hindus and Muslims by fighting a wrong that touched them equally.[12]

After the protest gathered steam, the leaders realised the power of salt as a symbol. Nehru remarked about the unprecedented popular response, "it seemed as though a spring had been suddenly released."[16]

Satyagraha

Main article: Satyagraha

Gandhi had a long-standing commitment to nonviolent civil disobedience, which he termed *satyagraha*, as the basis for achieving Indian sovereignty and self-rule .[20][21] Referring to the relationship between *satyagraha* and *Purna Swaraj*, Gandhi saw "an inviolable connection between the means and the end as there is between the seed and the tree".[22] He wrote, "If the means employed are impure, the change will not be in the direction of progress but very likely in the opposite. Only a change brought about in our political condition by pure means can lead to real progress."[23]

Satyagraha is a synthesis of the Sanskrit words *Satya* (truth) and *Agraha* (insistence on). For Gandhi, satyagraha went far beyond mere "passive resistance" and became strength in practising nonviolent methods. In his words:

Truth (satya) implies love, and firmness (agraha) engenders and therefore serves as a synonym for force. I thus began to call the Indian movement Satyagraha, that is to say, the Force which is born of Truth and Love or nonviolence, and gave up the use of the phrase "passive resistance", in connection with it, so much so that even in English writing we often avoided it and used instead the word "satyagraha" ...[24]

His first significant attempt in India at leading mass satyagraha was the non-cooperation movement from 1920 to 1922. Even though it succeeded in raising millions of Indians in protest against the British-created Rowlatt Acts, violence broke out at Chauri Chaura, where a mob killed 22 unarmed policemen. Gandhi suspended the protest, against the opposition of other Congress members. He decided that Indians were not yet ready for successful nonviolent resistance.[25] The Bardoli Satyagraha in 1928 was much more successful. It succeeded in paralysing the British government and winning significant concessions. More importantly, due to extensive press coverage, it scored a propaganda victory out of all proportion to its size.[26] Gandhi later claimed that success at Bardoli confirmed his belief in Satyagraha and Swaraj: "It is only gradually that we shall come to know the importance of the victory gained at Bardoli ... Bardoli has shown the way and cleared it. Swaraj lies on that route, and that alone is the cure ..."[27][28] Gandhi recruited heavily from the Bardoli Satyagraha participants for the Dandi march, which passed through many of the same villages that took part in the Bardoli protests.[29] This revolt gained momentum and had support from all parts of India

Preparing to march

Gandhi on the Salt March

On 5 February, newspapers reported that Gandhi would begin civil disobedience by defying the salt laws. The salt satyagraha would begin on 12 March and end in Dandi with Gandhi breaking the Salt Act on 6 April.[30] Gandhi chose 6 April to launch the mass breaking of the salt laws for a symbolic reason—it was the first day of "National Week", begun in 1919 when Gandhi conceived of the national hartal (strike) against the Rowlatt Act.[31]

Gandhi prepared the worldwide media for the march by issuing regular statements from Sabarmati, at his regular prayer meetings and through direct contact with the press. Expectations were heightened by his repeated statements anticipating arrest, and his increasingly dramatic language as the hour approached: "We are entering upon a life and death struggle, a holy war; we are performing an all-embracing sacrifice in which we wish to offer ourselves as oblation."[32] Correspondents from dozens of Indian, European, and American newspapers, along with film companies, responded to the drama and began covering the event.[33]

For the march itself, Gandhi wanted the strictest discipline and adherence to satyagraha and ahimsa. For that reason, he recruited the marchers not from Congress Party members, but from the residents of his own ashram, who were trained in Gandhi's strict standards of discipline.[34] The 24-day march would pass through 4 districts and 48 villages. The route of the march, along with each evening's stopping place, was planned based on recruitment potential, past contacts, and timing. Gandhi sent scouts to each village ahead of the march so he could plan his talks at each resting place, based on the needs of the local residents.[35] Events at each village were scheduled and publicised in Indian and foreign press.[36]

On 2 March 1930 Gandhi wrote to the Viceroy, Lord Irwin, offering to stop the march if Irwin met eleven demands, including reduction of land revenue assessments, cutting military spending, imposing a tariff on foreign cloth, and abolishing the salt tax.[12][37] His strongest appeal to Irwin regarded the salt tax:

If my letter makes no appeal to your heart, on the eleventh day of this month I shall proceed with such co-workers of the Ashram as I can take, to disregard the provisions of the Salt Laws. I regard this tax to be the most iniquitous of all from the poor man's standpoint. As the sovereignty and self-rule movement is essentially for the poorest in the land, the beginning will be made with this evil.[38]

As mentioned earlier, the Viceroy held any prospect of a "salt protest" in disdain. After he ignored the letter and refused to meet with Gandhi, the march was set in motion.[39] Gandhi remarked, "On bended knees I asked for bread and I have received stone instead."[40] The eve of the march brought thousands of Indians to Sabarmati to hear Gandhi speak at the regular evening prayer. An American academic writing for The Nation reported that "60,000 persons gathered on the bank of the river to hear Gandhi's call to arms. This call to arms was perhaps the most remarkable call to war that has ever been made."[41][42]

March to Dandi

File:Salt March.ogv

Original footage of Gandhi and his followers marching to Dandi in the Salt Satyagraha

On 12 March 1930, Gandhi and 80 satyagrahis, many of whom were from scheduled castes, set out on foot for the coastal village of Dandi, Gujarat, over 390 kilometres (240 mi) from their starting point at Sabarmati Ashram.[30] The Salt March was also called the **White Flowing River** because all the people were joining the procession wearing white khadi.

According to *The Statesman*, the official government newspaper which usually played down the size of crowds at Gandhi's functions, 100,000 people crowded the road that separated Sabarmati from Ahmadabad.[43][44] The first day's march of 21 kilometres (13 mi) ended in the village of Aslali, where Gandhi spoke to a crowd of about 4,000.[45] At Aslali, and the other villages that the march passed through, volunteers collected donations, registered new satyagrahis, and received resignations from village officials who chose to end co-operation with British rule.[46]

As they entered each village, crowds greeted the marchers, beating drums and cymbals. Gandhi gave speeches attacking the salt tax as inhuman, and the salt satyagraha as a "poor man's struggle". Each night they slept in the open. The only thing that was asked of the villagers was food and water to wash with. Gandhi felt that this would bring the poor into the struggle for sovereignty and self-rule, necessary for eventual victory.[47]

Thousands of satyagrahis and leaders like Sarojini Naidu joined him. Every day, more and more people joined the march, until the procession of marchers became at least two miles long.[48] To keep up their spirits, the marchers used to sing the Hindu bhajan Raghupati Raghava Raja Ram while walking.[49] At Surat, they were greeted by 30,000 people. When they reached the railhead at Dandi, more than 50,000 were gathered. Gandhi gave interviews and wrote articles along the way. Foreign journalists and three Bombay cinema companies shooting newsreel footage turned Gandhi into a household name in Europe and America (at the end of 1930, *Time* magazine made him "Man of the Year").[47] The *New York Times* wrote almost daily about the Salt March, including two front-page articles on 6 and 7 April.[50] Near the end of the march, Gandhi declared, "I want world sympathy in this battle of right against might."[51]

Upon arriving at the seashore on 5 April, Gandhi was interviewed by an Associated Press reporter. He stated:

I cannot withhold my compliments from the government for the policy of complete non interference adopted by them throughout the march .... I wish I could believe this non-interference was due to any real change of heart or policy. The wanton disregard shown by them to popular feeling in the Legislative Assembly and their high-handed action leave no room for doubt that the policy of heartless exploitation of India is to be persisted in at any cost, and so the only interpretation I can put upon this non-interference is that the British Government, powerful though it is, is sensitive to world opinion which will not tolerate repression of extreme political agitation which civil disobedience undoubtedly is, so long as disobedience remains civil and therefore necessarily non-violent .... It remains to be seen whether the Government will tolerate as they have tolerated the march, the actual breach of the salt laws by countless people from tomorrow.[52][53]

The following morning, after a prayer, Gandhi raised a lump of salty mud and declared, "With this, I am shaking the foundations of the British Empire."[19] He then boiled it in seawater, producing illegal salt. He implored his thousands of followers to likewise begin making salt along the seashore, "wherever it is convenient" and to instruct villagers in making illegal, but necessary, salt.[54]

First 80 Marchers

79 Marchers accompanied Gandhi on his march. Most of them were between the ages of 20 and 30. These men hailed from almost all parts of the country. The march gathered more people as it gained momentum, but the following list of names were the first 79 marchers who were with Gandhi from the beginning of the Dandi March until the end. Most of them simply dispersed after the march was over.[55][56]

Number

Name

Age

Province (British India)

State (Republic of India)

1

Mohandas Karamchand Gandhi

61

Princely State of Porbandar

Gujarat

2

Pyarelal Nayyar

30

Punjab
Punjab
3
Chhaganlal Naththubhai Joshi
35
Unknown Princely State
Gujarat
4
Pandit Narayan Moreshwar Khare
42
Bombay
Maharashtra
5
Ganpatrav Godshe
25
Bombay
Maharashtra
6
Prathviraj Lakshmidas Ashar
19
Kutch
Gujarat
7
Mahavir Giri
20
Princely State of Nepal
8
Bal Dattatreya Kalelkar
18
Bombay
Maharashtra
9
Jayanti Nathubhai Parekh
19
Unknown Princely State
Gujarat
10
Rasik Desai
19
Unknown Princely State
Gujarat
11
Vitthal Liladhar Thakkar
16
Unknown Princely State
Gujarat
12
Harakhji Ramjibhai

18
Unknown Princely State
Gujarat
13
Tansukh Pranshankar Bhatt
20
Unknown Princely State
Gujarat
14
Kantilal Harilal Gandhi
20
Unknown Princely State
Gujarat
15
Chhotubhai Khushalbhai Patel
22
Unknown Princely State
Gujarat
16
Valjibhai Govindji Desai
35
Unknown Princely State
Gujarat
17
Pannalal Balabhai Jhaveri
20
Gujarat
18
Abbas Varteji
20
Gujarat
19
Punjabhai Shah
25
Gujarat
20
Madhavjibhai Thakkar
40
Kutch
Gujarat
21
Naranjibhai
22
Kutch
Gujarat
22
Maganbhai Vora
25

Kutch
Gujarat
23
Dungarsibhai
27
Kutch
Gujarat
24
Somalal Pragjibhai Patel
25
Gujarat
25
Hasmukhram Jakabar
25
Gujarat
26
Daudbhai
25
Gujarat
27
Ramjibhai Vankar
45
Gujarat
28
Dinkarrai Pandya
30
Gujarat
29
Dwarkanath
30
Maharashtra
30
Gajanan Khare
25
Maharashtra
31
Jethalal Ruparel
25
Kutch
Gujarat
32
Govind Harkare
25
Maharashtra
33
Pandurang
22
Maharashtra

34
Vinayakrao Aapte
33
Maharashtra
35
Ramdhirrai
30
United Provinces
36
Bhanushankar Dave
22
Gujarat
37
Munshilal
25
United Provinces
38
Raghavan
25
Madras Presidency
Kerala
39
Ravjibhai Nathalal Patel
30
Gujarat
40
Shivabhai Gokhalbhai Patel
27
Gujarat
41
Shankarbhai Bhikabhai Patel
20
Gujarat
42
Jashbhai Ishwarbhai Patel
20
Gujarat
43
Sumangal Prakash
25
United Provinces
44
Thevarthundiyil Titus
25
Madras Presidency
Kerala
45
Krishna Nair

25
Madras Presidency
Kerala
46
Tapan Nair
25
Madras Presidency
Kerala
47
Haridas Varjivandas Gandhi
25
Gujarat
48
Chimanlal Narsilal Shah
25
Gujarat
49
Shankaran
25
Madras Presidency
Kerala
50
Subhramanyam
25
Andhra Pradesh
51
Ramaniklal Maganlal Modi
38
Gujarat
52
Madanmohan Chaturvedi
27
Rajputana
Rajasthan
53
Harilal Mahimtura
27
Maharashtra
54
Motibas Das
20
Odisha
55
Haridas Muzumdar
25
Gujarat
56
Anand Hingorini

24
Sindh
Sindh (Pakistan)
57
Mahadev Martand
18
Karnataka
58
Jayantiprasad
30
United Provinces
59
Hariprasad
20
United Provinces
60
Anugrah Narain Sinha
20
Bihar
61
Keshav Chitre
25
Maharashtra
62
Ambalal Shankarbhai Patel
30
Gujarat
63
Vishnu Pant
25
Maharashtra
64
Premraj
35
Punjab
65
Durgesh Chandra Das
44
Bengal
Bengal
66
Madhavlal Shah
27
Gujarat
67
Jyotiram
30
United Provinces

68

Surajbhan

34

Punjab

69

Bhairav Dutt

25

United Provinces

70

Lalji Parmar

25

Gujarat

71

Ratnaji Boria

18

Gujarat

72

Vishnu Sharma

30

Maharashtra

73

Chintamani Shastri

40

Maharashtra

74

Narayan Dutt

24

Rajputana
Rajasthan

75

Manilal Mohandas Gandhi

38

Gujarat

76

Surendra

30

United Provinces

77

Hari Krishna Mohoni

42

Maharashtra

78

Puratan Buch

25

Gujarat

79

Kharag Bahadur Singh Giri

25

Princely State of Nepal
80
Shri Jagat Narayan
50
Uttar Pradesh
A memorial has been created inside the campus of IIT Bombay honouring these Satyagrahis.[57]

The Schedule of the March[edit]

Date

Day
Mid Day Halt
Night Halt
Miles

12-03-1930
Wednesday
Chandola Talao
Aslali
13
13-03-1930
Thursday
Bareja
Navagam
9
14-03-1930
Friday
Vasna
Matar
10
15-03-1930
Saturday
Dabhan
Nadiad
15
16-03-1930
Sunday
Boriavi
Anand
11
17-03-1930
Monday
Rest Day at Anand
0
18-03-1930
Tuesday
Napa
Borsad
11

19-03-1930
Wednesday
Ras
Kankarpura
12
20-03-1930
Thursday
Bank of Mahisagar
Kareli
11
21-03-1930
Friday
Gajera
Ankhi
11
22-03-1930
Saturday
Jambusar
Amod]
12
23-03-1930
Sunday
Buva
Samni
12
24-03-1930
Monday
Rest Day at Samni
0
25-03-1930
Tuesday
Tralsa
Derol
10
26-03-1930
Wednesday
Bharuch
Ankleshwar
13
27-03-1930
Thursday
Sanjod
Mangarol
12
28-03-1930
Friday
Ryma
Umarachi

10
29-03-1930
Saturday
Erthan
Bhatgam
10
30-03-1930
Sunday
Sandhier
Delad
12
31-03-1930
Monday
Rest Day at Delad
0
01-04-1930
Tuesday
Chaprabhata
Surat
11
02-04-1930
Wednesday
Dindoli
Vanz
12
03-04-1930
Thursday
Dhaman
Navasari
13
04-04-1930
Friday
Vijalpur
Karadi
9
05-04-1930
Saturday
karadi-Matwad
Dandi
4
[58]

Mass civil disobedience

Gandhi at a public rally during the Salt Satyagraha.

Mass civil disobedience spread throughout India as millions broke the salt laws by making salt or buying illegal salt.[19] Salt was sold illegally all over the coast of India. A pinch of salt made by Gandhi himself sold for 1,600 rupees (equivalent to $750 at the time). In reaction, the British government arrested over sixty thousand people by the end of the month.[52]

What had begun as a Salt Satyagraha quickly grew into a mass Satyagraha.[59] British cloth and goods were boycotted. Unpopular forest laws were defied in the Maharashtra, Karnataka and Central Provinces. Gujarati peasants refused to pay tax, under threat of losing their crops and land. In Midnapore, Bengalis took part by refusing to pay the chowkidar tax.[60] The British responded with more laws, including censorship of correspondence and declaring the Congress and its associate organisations illegal. None of those measures slowed the civil disobedience movement.[61]

There were outbreaks of violence in Calcutta (now spelled Kolkata), Karachi, and Gujarat. Unlike his suspension of satyagraha after violence broke out during the Non-co-operation movement, this time Gandhi was "unmoved". Appealing for violence to end, at the same time Gandhi honoured those killed in Chittagong and congratulated their parents "for the finished sacrifices of their sons ... A warrior's death is never a matter for sorrow."[62]

During the first phase of the civil disobedience movement from 1929 to 1931 there was a Labour government in power in Britain. The beatings at Dharasana, the shootings at Peshawar, the floggings and hangings at Solapur, the mass arrests, and much else were all presided over by a Labour prime minister, Ramsay MacDonald and his secretary of state, William Wedgwood Benn. The government was also complicit in a sustained attack on trade unionism in India,[63] an attack that Sumit Sarkar has described as "a massive capitalist and government counter-offensive" against workers' rights.[64]

Qissa Khwani Bazaar massacre

Khan Abdul Ghaffar Khan with Mahatma Gandhi
Main article: Qissa Khwani Bazaar massacre

In Peshawar, satyagraha was led by a Muslim Pashto disciple of Gandhi, Ghaffar Khan, who had trained 50,000 nonviolent activists called Khudai Khidmatgar.[65] On 23 April 1930, Ghaffar Khan was arrested. A crowd of Khudai Khidmatgar gathered in Peshawar's Qissa Kahani (Storytellers) Bazaar. The British ordered troops of 2/18 battalion of Royal Garhwal Rifles to open fire with machine guns on the unarmed crowd, killing an estimated 200–250.[66] The Pashtun satyagrahis acted in accord with their training in nonviolence, willingly facing bullets as the troops fired on them.[67] One British Indian Army Soldier Chandra Singh Garhwali and troops of the renowned Royal Garhwal Rifles, refused to fire at the crowds. The entire platoon was arrested and many received heavy penalties, including life imprisonment.[66]

Vedaranyam salt march

C. Rajagopalachari leading the march
Main article: Vedaranyam March

While Gandhi marched along India's west coast, his close associate C. Rajagopalachari, who would later become sovereign India's first Governor-General, organized the Vedaranyam salt march in parallel on the east coast. His group started from Tiruchirappalli, in Madras Presidency (now part of Tamil Nadu), to the coastal village of Vedaranyam. After making illegal salt there, he too was arrested by the British.[16]

Women in civil disobedience[edit]

The civil disobedience in 1930 marked the first time women became mass participants in the struggle for freedom. Thousands of women, from large cities to small villages, became active participants in satyagraha.[68] Gandhi had asked that only men take part in the salt march, but eventually women began manufacturing and selling salt throughout India. It was clear that though only men were allowed within the march, that both men and women were expected to forward work that would help dissolve the salt laws.[69] Usha Mehta, an early Gandhian activist, remarked that "Even our old aunts and great-aunts and grandmothers used to bring pitchers of salt water to their houses and manufacture illegal salt. And then they would shout at the top of their voices: 'We have broken the salt law!'"[70] The growing number of women in the fight for sovereignty and self-rule was a "new and serious feature" according to Lord Irwin. A government report on the involvement of women stated "thousands of them emerged ... from the seclusion of their homes ... in order to join Congress demonstrations and assist in picketing: and their presence on these occasions made the work the police was required to perform particularly unpleasant."[71] Though women did become involved in the march, it was clear that Gandhi saw women as still playing a secondary role within the movement, but created the beginning of a push for women to be more involved in the future.[69]

"Sarojini Naidu was among the most visible leaders (male or female) of pre-independent India. As president of the Indian National Congress and the first woman governor of free India, she was a fervent advocate for India, avidly mobilizing support for the Indian independence movement. She was also the first woman to be arrested in the salt march."[*attribution needed*][72]

Impact[edit]

British documents show that the British government was shaken by satyagraha. Nonviolent protest left the British confused about whether or not to jail Gandhi. John Court Curry, a British police officer stationed in India, wrote in his memoirs that he felt nausea every time he dealt with Congress demonstrations in 1930. Curry and others in British government, including Wedgwood Benn, Secretary of State for India, preferred fighting violent rather than nonviolent opponents.[71]

Dharasana Satyagraha and aftermath

Gandhi himself avoided further active involvement after the march, though he stayed in close contact with the developments throughout India. He created a temporary ashram near Dandi. From there, he urged women followers in Bombay (now spelled Mumbai) to picket liquor shops and foreign cloth. He said that "a bonfire should be made of foreign cloth. Schools and colleges should become empty."[62]

For his next major action, Gandhi decided on a raid of the Dharasana Salt Works in Gujarat, 25 miles (40 km) south of Dandi. He wrote to Lord Irwin, again telling him of his plans. Around midnight of 4 May, as Gandhi was sleeping on a cot in a mango grove, the District Magistrate of Surat drove up with two Indian officers and thirty heavily armed constables.[73] He was arrested under an 1827 regulation calling for the jailing of people engaged in unlawful activities, and held without trial near Poona (now Pune).[74]

Main article: Dharasana Satyagraha

The Dharasana Satyagraha went ahead as planned, with Abbas Tyabji, a seventy-six-year-old retired judge, leading the march with Gandhi's wife Kasturba at his side. Both were arrested before reaching Dharasana and sentenced to three months in prison. After their arrests, the march continued under the leadership of Sarojini Naidu, a woman poet and freedom fighter, who warned the satyagrahis, "You must not use any violence under any circumstances. You will be beaten, but you must not resist: you must not even raise a hand to ward off blows." Soldiers began clubbing the satyagrahis with steel tipped lathis in an incident that attracted international attention.[75] United Press correspondent Webb Miller reported that:

Not one of the marchers even raised an arm to fend off the blows. They went down like ten-pins. From where I stood I heard the sickening whacks of the clubs on unprotected skulls. The waiting crowd of watchers groaned and sucked in their breaths in sympathetic pain at every blow. Those struck down fell sprawling, unconscious or writhing in pain with fractured skulls or broken shoulders. In two or three minutes the ground was quilted with bodies. Great patches of blood widened on their white clothes. The survivors without breaking ranks silently and doggedly marched on until struck down ... Finally the police became enraged by the non-resistance ... They commenced savagely kicking the seated men in the abdomen and testicles. The injured men writhed and squealed in agony, which seemed to inflame the fury of the police ... The police then began dragging the sitting men by the arms or feet, sometimes for a hundred yards, and throwing them into ditches. [76]

Vithalbhai Patel, former Speaker of the Assembly, watched the beatings and remarked, "All hope of reconciling India with the British Empire is lost forever."[77] Miller's first attempts at telegraphing the story to his publisher in England were censored by the British telegraph operators in India. Only after threatening to expose British censorship was his story allowed to pass. The story appeared in 1,350 newspapers throughout the world and was read into the official record of the United States Senate by Senator John J. Blaine.[78]

Salt Satyagraha succeeded in drawing the attention of the world. Millions saw the newsreels showing the march. *Time* declared Gandhi its 1930 Man of the Year, comparing Gandhi's march to the sea "to defy Britain's salt tax as some New Englanders once defied a British tea tax".[79] Civil disobedience continued until early 1931, when Gandhi was finally released from prison to hold talks with Irwin. It was the first time the two held talks on equal terms,[80] and resulted in the Gandhi–Irwin Pact. The talks would lead to the Second Round Table Conference at the end of 1931.

Long-term effect

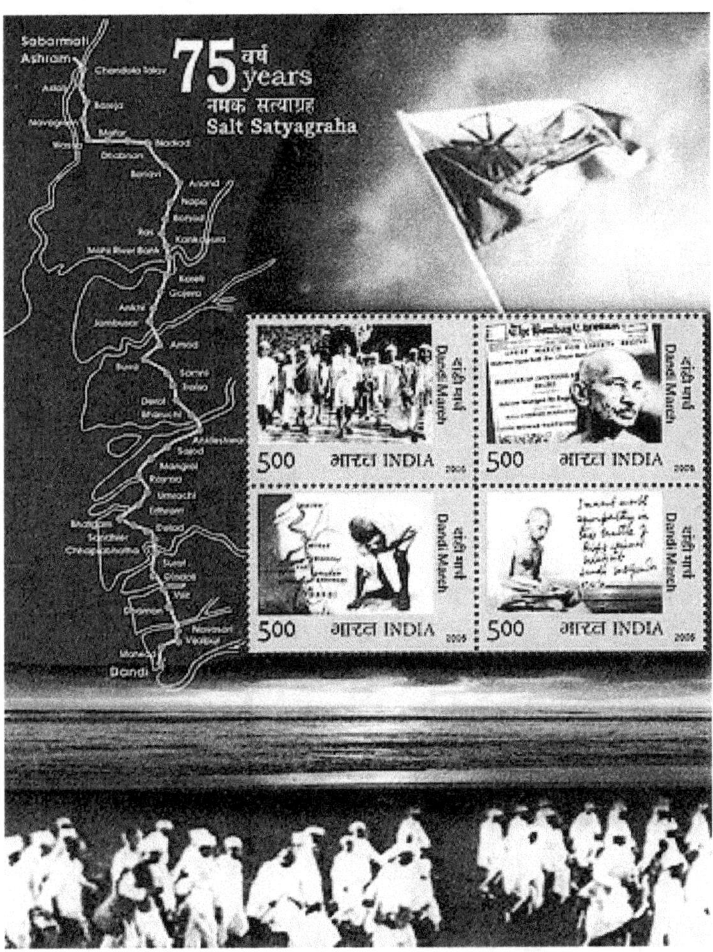

A 2005 stamp sheet of India dedicated to the Salt March

Salt Satyagraha produced scant progress toward dominion status or self-rule for India, and did not win any major concessions from the British.[81] It also failed to attract Muslim support.[82] Congress leaders decided to end satyagraha as official policy in 1934. Nehru and other Congress members drifted further apart from Gandhi, who withdrew from Congress to concentrate on his Constructive Programme, which included his efforts to end <u>untouchability</u> in the <u>Harijan</u> movement.[83] Even though British authorities were again in control by the mid-1930s, Indian, British, and world opinion increasingly began to recognise the legitimacy of claims by Gandhi and the Congress Party for sovereignty and self-rule .[84] The Satyagraha campaign of the 1930s also forced the British to recognise that their control of India depended entirely on the consent of the Indians – Salt Satyagraha was a significant step in the British losing that consent.[85]

Nehru considered the Salt Satyagraha the high-water mark of his association with Gandhi,[86] and felt that its lasting importance was in changing the attitudes of Indians:

Of course these movements exercised tremendous pressure on the British Government and shook the government machinery. But the real importance, to my mind, lay in the effect they had on our own people, and especially the village masses ... Non-cooperation dragged them out of the mire and gave them self-respect and self-reliance ... They acted courageously and did not submit so easily to unjust oppression; their outlook widened and they began to think a little in terms of India as a whole ... It was a remarkable transformation and the Congress, under Gandhi's leadership, must have the credit for it.[87]

More than thirty years later, Satyagraha and the March to Dandi exercised a strong influence on American civil rights activist <u>Martin Luther King Jr.</u>, and his fight for civil rights for blacks in the 1960s:

Like most people, I had heard of Gandhi, but I had never studied him seriously. As I read I became deeply fascinated by his campaigns of nonviolent resistance. I was particularly moved by his Salt March to the Sea and his numerous fasts. The whole concept of *Satyagraha* (*Satya* is truth which equals love, and *agraha* is force; *Satyagraha*, therefore, means truth force or love force) was profoundly significant to me. As I delved deeper into the philosophy of Gandhi, my skepticism concerning the power of love gradually diminished, and I came to see for the first time its potency in the area of social reform.[8]

Re-enactment in 2005

To commemorate the Great Salt March, the Mahatma Gandhi Foundation re-enacted the Salt March on its 75th anniversary, in its exact historical schedule and route followed by the Mahatma and his band of 80 marchers. The event was known as the "International Walk for Justice and Freedom". What started as a personal pilgrimage for Mahatma Gandhi's great-grandson Tushar Gandhi turned into an international event with 900 registered participants from 9 nations and on a daily basis the numbers swelled to a couple of thousands. There was extensive reportage in the international media.

The start of the march on 12 March 2005 in Ahmedabad was attended by Sonia Gandhi, Chairperson of the United Progressive Alliance, as well as several Indian Cabinet Ministers, many of whom joined the march at different locations along the route and walked part of the way.

The participants halted at Dandi on the night of 5 April, with the commemoration ending on 7 April. At the finale in Dandi, the prime minister of India, Dr Manmohan Singh, greeted the marchers and promised to build an appropriate monument at Dandi to commemorate the marchers and the historical event. The route from Sabarmati Ashram to Dandi has now been christened as the Dandi Path and has been declared a historical heritage route.[88][89]

Series of commemorative stamps were issued in 1980 and 2005, on the 50th and 75th anniversaries of the Dandi March.[90]

Memorial

The National Salt Satyagraha Memorial, a memorial museum, dedicated to the event was opened in Dandi on 30 January 2019.

CH 8 BATTLE OF PLASSEY

Battle of Plassey

Battle of Plassey

Part of the Seven Years' War
An oil-on-canvas painting depicting the meeting of Mir Jafar and Robert Clive after the Battle of Plassey by Francis Hayman

Lord Clive meeting with Mir Jafar after the Battle of Plassey, oil on canvas (Francis Hayman, c. 1762)

Date
23 June 1757
Location

Palashi, Bengal Subah

Coordinates: 23.80°N 88.25°E

Result

British victory

Territorial changes

Bengal annexed by the British East India Company.

Belligerents

Great Britain

- East India Company

Bengal Subah

Kingdom of France

the Mughal Empire.svg

- French East India Company

Commanders and leaders

- Colonel Robert Clive
- Major Kilpatrick
- Major Grant
- Major Eyre Coote
- Captain Gaupp
- Capt. William Jennings

- Nawab Siraj ud-Daulah   Executed
- Diwan Mohanlal
- Mir Madan †
- Mir Jafar Ali Khan (*defector*)
- Yar Lutuf Khan (*defector*)
- Rai Durlabh (*defector*)

St. Frais

Strength

East India Company:

- 750 British European soldiers
- 100 Topasses
- 2,100 Indian sepoys
- 100 gunners
- 50 sailors
- 8 cannon (six 68-pounders and 2 howitzers)

defectors:

- 15,000 cavalry of Mir Jafar
- 35,000 infantry

Mughal Empire:

- 7,000 infantry
- 5,000 cavalry of Siraj ud-Daulah
- 35,000 infantry (defected)
- 15,000 cavalry of Mir Jafar (defected)
- 53 field pieces (mostly 32, 24 and 18-pounder pieces)

France :

- 50 artillerymen (6 field pieces)

Casualties and losses

- 22 killed
- 50 wounded

500 killed and wounded

show

- v
- t
- e

Third Carnatic War

The **Battle of Plassey** was a decisive victory of the British East India Company over the Nawab of Bengal and his French[1] allies on 22 June 1757, under the leadership of Robert Clive. The battle consolidated the Company's presence in Bengal, which later expanded to cover much of India over the next hundred years.

The battle took place at Palashi (Anglicised version: *Plassey*) on the banks of the Hooghly River, about 150 kilometres (93 mi) north of Calcutta and south of Murshidabad, then capital of Bengal (now in Murshidabad district in West Bengal). The belligerents were the Nawab Siraj-ud-Daulah, the last independent Nawab of Bengal, and the British East India Company. Siraj-ud-Daulah had become the Nawab of Bengal the year before, and he ordered the English to stop the extension of their fortification. Robert Clive bribed Mir Jafar, the commander-in-chief of the Nawab's army, and also promised him to make him Nawab of Bengal. Clive defeated Siraj-ud-Daulah at Plassey in 1757 and captured Calcutta.[2]

The battle was preceded by an attack on British-controlled Calcutta by Nawab Siraj-ud-Daulah and the Black Hole massacre. The British sent reinforcements under Colonel Robert Clive and Admiral Charles Watson from Madras to Bengal and recaptured Calcutta. Clive then seized the initiative to capture the French fort of Chandernagar.[3] Tensions and suspicions between Siraj-ud-daulah and the British culminated in the Battle of Plassey. The battle was waged during the Seven Years' War (1756–1763), and, in a mirror of their European rivalry, the French East India Company (*La Compagnie des Indes Orientales*)[1] sent a small contingent to fight against the

British. Siraj-ud-Daulah had a numerically superior force and made his stand at Plassey. The British, worried about being outnumbered, formed a conspiracy with Siraj-ud-Daulah's demoted army chief Mir Jafar, along with others such as Yar Lutuf Khan, Jagat Seths (Mahtab Chand and Swarup Chand), Umichand and Rai Durlabh. Mir Jafar, Rai Durlabh and Yar Lutuf Khan thus assembled their troops near the battlefield but made no move to actually join the battle. Siraj-ud-Daulah's army with 50,000 soldiers, 40 cannons and 10 war elephants was defeated by 3,000 soldiers of Col. Robert Clive, owing to the flight of Siraj-ud-Daulah from the battlefield and the inactivity of the conspirators. The battle ended in 11 hours.

This is judged to be one of the pivotal battles in the control of Indian subcontinent by the colonial powers. The British now wielded enormous influence over the Nawab and consequently acquired significant concessions for previous losses and revenue from trade. The British further used this revenue to increase their military might and push the other European colonial powers such as the Dutch and the French out of South Asia, thus expanding the British Empire.

Contents

Background

<u>A map of the Indian subcontinent depicting the European settlements in India in the period from 1501 to 1739</u>

European settlements in India from 1501 to 1739.

The <u>British East India Company</u> had a strong presence in India with the three main stations of <u>Fort St. George</u> in <u>Madras</u>, <u>Fort William</u> in <u>Calcutta</u> and <u>Bombay Castle</u> in western India.

These stations were independent presidencies governed by a president and a council, appointed by the Court of Directors in England. The British adopted a policy of allying themselves with various princes and Nawabs, promising security against usurpers and rebels. The Nawabs often gave them concessions in return for the security.

By the 18th century all rivalry had ceased between the British East India Company and the <u>Dutch</u> or <u>Portuguese</u> counterparts. The French had also established an <u>East India Company</u> under <u>Louis XIV</u> and had two important stations in India – <u>Chandernagar</u> in <u>Bengal</u> and <u>Pondicherry</u> on the <u>Carnatic</u> coast, both governed by the presidency of Pondicherry. The French were a late comer in India trade, but they quickly established themselves in India and were poised to overtake Britain for control.[4][5]

Carnatic Wars

The <u>War of the Austrian Succession</u> (1740–1748) marked the beginning of the power struggle between Britain and France and of European military ascendancy and political intervention in the Indian subcontinent. In September 1746, <u>Mahé de La Bourdonnais</u> landed off <u>Madras</u> with a naval squadron and laid <u>siege to the port city</u>. The defences of Madras were weak and the <u>garrison</u> sustained a bombardment of three days before surrendering. The terms of the surrender agreed by Bourdonnais provided for the settlement to be ransomed back for a cash payment by the British East India Company. However, this concession was opposed by <u>Joseph François Dupleix</u>, the governor general of the Indian possessions of the <u>Compagnie des Indes Orientales</u>. When Bourdonnais left India in October, Dupleix reneged on the agreement. The Nawab of the Carnatic <u>Anwaruddin Khan</u> intervened in support of the British and the combined forces advanced to retake Madras, but despite vast superiority in numbers, the army was easily <u>crushed</u> by the French. As retaliation to the loss of Madras, the British, under Major <u>Lawrence</u> and Admiral <u>Boscawen</u>, laid <u>siege to Pondicherry</u> but were forced to raise it after thirty-one days. The <u>Treaty of Aix-la-Chapelle</u> in 1748 forced Dupleix to yield Madras back to the British in return for <u>Louisbourg</u> and <u>Cape Breton Island</u> in North America.[4][6]

The Mughal Empire's Nawab of Bengal Alivardi Khan adopted strict attitudes towards European mercantile companies in Bengal.

The Treaty of Aix-La-Chapelle prevented direct hostilities between the two powers but soon they were involved in indirect hostilities as the auxiliaries of the local princes in their feuds. The feud Dupleix chose was for the succession to the positions of the Nizam of the Deccan and the Nawab of the dependent Carnatic province. The British and the French both nominated their candidates for the two posts. In both cases, Dupleix's candidates usurped both thrones by manipulation and two assassinations. In mid-1751, the French candidate for the Nawab's post, Chanda Sahib, laid siege to the British candidate Wallajah's last stronghold Trichinopoly, where Wallajah was holed up with his British reinforcements. He was aided by a French force under Charles, Marquis de Bussy.[4][7]

On 1 September 1751, 280 Europeans and 300 sepoys under the command of Captain Robert Clive attacked and seized Arcot, the capital of the Carnatic, finding that the garrison had fled the night before. It was hoped that this would force Chanda Sahib to divert some of his troops to wrest the city back from the British. Chanda Sahib sent a force of 4,000 Indians under Raza Sahib and 150 Frenchmen. They besieged the fort and breached the walls in various places after several weeks. Clive sent out a message to Morari Rao, a Maratha chieftain who had received a subsidy to assist Wallajah and was encamped in the Mysore hills. Raza Sahib, learning of the imminent Maratha approach, sent a letter to Clive asking him to surrender in return for a large sum of money but this offer was refused. In the morning of 24 November, Raza Sahib tried to mount a final assault on the fort but was foiled in his attempt when his armoured elephants stampeded due to the British musketry. They tried to enter the fort through the breach several times but always repulsed with loss. The siege was raised the next day and Raza Sahib's forces fled from the scene, abandoning guns, ammunition and stores. With success at Arcot, Conjeeveram and Trichinopoly, the British secured the Carnatic and Wallajah succeeded to the throne of the Nawab in accordance with a treaty with the new French governor Godeheu.[8][9]

Alwardi Khan ascended to the throne of the Nawab of Bengal after his army attacked and captured the capital of Bengal, Murshidabad. Alivardi's attitude to the Europeans in Bengal is said to be strict. During his wars with the Marathas, he allowed the strengthening of fortifications by the Europeans and the construction of the Maratha Ditch in Calcutta by the British. On the other hand, he collected large amounts of money from them for the upkeep of his war. He was well-informed of the situation in southern India, where the British and the French had started a proxy war using the local princes and rulers. Alwardi did not wish such a situation to transpire in his province and thus exercised caution in his dealings with the Europeans. However, there was continual friction; the British always complained that they were prevented from the full enjoyment of the farman of 1717 issued by Farrukhsiyar. The British, however, protected subjects of the Nawab, gave passes to native traders to trade custom-free and levied large duties on goods coming to their districts – actions which were detrimental to the Nawab's revenue.[10]

In April 1756, Alwardi Khan died and was succeeded by his twenty-three-year-old grandson, Siraj-ud-daulah. His personality was said to be a combination of a ferocious temper and a feeble understanding. He was particularly suspicious of the large profits made by the European companies in India. When the British and the French started improving their fortifications in anticipation of another war between them, he immediately ordered them to stop such activities as they had been done without permission.[11] When the British refused to cease their constructions, the Nawab led a detachment of 3,000 men to surround the fort and factory of Cossimbazar and took several British officials as prisoners, before moving to Calcutta.[12] The defences of Calcutta were weak and negligible. The garrison consisted of only 180 soldiers, 50 European volunteers, 60 European militia, 150 Armenian and Portuguese militia, 35 European artillery-men and 40 volunteers from ships and was pitted against the Nawab's force of nearly 50,000 infantry and cavalry. The city was occupied on 16 June by Siraj's force and the fort surrendered after a brief siege on 20 June.[13][14][15][16][17]

The prisoners who were captured at the siege of Calcutta were transferred by Siraj to the care of the officers of his guard, who confined them to the common dungeon of Fort William known as The Black Hole. This dungeon, 18 by 14 feet (5.5 m × 4.3 m) in size with two small windows, had 146 prisoners thrust into it – originally employed by the British to hold only six prisoners. On 21 June, the doors of the dungeon were opened and only 23 of the 146 walked out, the rest died of asphyxiation, heat exhaustion and delirium.[18] It appears that the Nawab was unaware of the conditions in which his prisoners were held which resulted in the unfortunate deaths of most of the prisoners. Meanwhile, the Nawab's army and navy were busy plundering the city of Calcutta and the other British factories in the surrounding areas.[19][20][21][22]

When news of the fall of Calcutta broke in Madras on 16 August 1756, the Council immediately sent out an expeditionary force under Colonel Clive and Admiral Watson. A letter from the Council of Fort St. George, states that "the object of the expedition was not merely to re-establish the British settlements in Bengal, but also to obtain ample recognition of the Company's privileges and reparation for its losses" without the risk of war. It also states that any signs of dissatisfaction and ambition among the Nawab's subjects must be supported.[23] Clive assumed command of the land forces, consisting of 900 Europeans and 1500 sepoys while Watson commanded a naval squadron. The fleet entered the Hooghly River in December and met with the fugitives of Calcutta and the surrounding areas, including the principal Members of the Council, at the village of Falta on 15 December. The Members of Council formed a Select Committee of direction. On 29 December, the force dislodged the enemy from the fort of Budge Budge. Clive and Watson then moved against Calcutta on 2 January 1757 and the garrison of 500 men surrendered after offering a scanty resistance.[24] With Calcutta recaptured, the Council was reinstated and a plan of action against the Nawab was prepared. The fortifications of Fort William were strengthened and a defensive position was prepared in the north-east of the city.[25][22][26]

Bengal campaign

Robert Clive (1773), by Nathaniel Dance-Holland.

On 9 January 1757, a force of 650 men under Captain Coote and Major Kilpatrick stormed and sacked the town of Hooghly, 23 miles (37 km) north of Calcutta.[27] On learning of this attack, the Nawab raised his army and marched on Calcutta, arriving with the main body on 3 February and encamping beyond the Maratha Ditch. Siraj set up his headquarters in Omichund's garden. A small body of their army attacked the northern suburbs of the town but were beaten back by a detachment under Lieutenant Lebeaume placed there, returning with fifty prisoners.[28][29][30][31][32]

Clive decided to launch a surprise attack on the Nawab's camp on the morning of 4 February. At midnight, a force of 600 sailors, a battalion of 650 Europeans, 100 artillery-men, 800 sepoys and 6 six-pounders approached the Nawab's camp. At 6:00, under the cover of a thick fog, the vanguard came upon the Nawab's advanced guard, who after firing with their matchlocks and rockets, ran away. They continued forward for some distance till they were opposite Omichund's garden, when they heard the galloping of cavalry on their right. The cavalry came within 30 yards (27 m) of the British force before the line gave fire, killing many and dispersing the rest. The fog hampered visibility beyond walking distance. Hence, the line moved slowly, infantry and artillery firing on either side randomly. Clive had intended to use a narrow raised causeway, south of the garden, to attack the Nawab's quarters in the garden. The Nawab's troops had barricaded the passage. At about 9:00, as the fog began to lift, the troops were overwhelmed by the discharge of two pieces of heavy cannon from across the Maratha Ditch by the Nawab's artillery. The British troops were assailed on all sides by cavalry and musket-fire. The Nawab troops then made for a bridge a mile further on, crossed the Maratha Ditch and reached Calcutta. The total casualties of Clive's force were 57 killed and 137 wounded. The Nawab's army lost 22 officers of distinction, 600 common men, 4 elephants, 500 horses, some camels and a great number of bullocks. The attack scared the Nawab into concluding the Treaty of Alinagar with the Company on 5 February, agreeing to restore the Company's factories, allow the fortification of Calcutta and restoring former privileges. The Nawab withdrew his army back to his capital, Murshidabad.[33][34][35][36][37]

Concerned by the approach of de Bussy to Bengal and the Seven Years' War in Europe, the Company turned its attention to the French threat in Bengal. Clive planned to capture the French town of Chandernagar, 20 miles (32 km) north of Calcutta. Clive needed to know whose side the Nawab would intervene on if he attacked Chandernagar. The Nawab sent evasive replies and Clive construed this to be assent to the attack.[38] Clive commenced hostilities on the town and fort of Chandernagar on 14 March. The French had set up defences on the roads leading to the fort and had sunk several ships in the river channel to prevent passage of the men of war. The garrison consisted of 600 Europeans and 300 sepoys. The French expected assistance from the Nawab's forces from Hooghly, but the governor of Hooghly, Nandkumar had been bribed to remain inactive and prevent the Nawab's reinforcement of Chandernagar. The fort was well-defended, but when Admiral Watson's squadron forced the blockade in the channel on 23 March, a fierce cannonade ensued with aid from two batteries on the shore. The naval squadron suffered greatly due to musket-fire from the fort. At 9:00 on 24 March, a flag of truce was shown by the French and by 15:00, the capitulation concluded. After plundering Chandernagar, Clive decided to ignore his orders to return to Madras and remain in Bengal. He moved his army to the north of the town of Hooghly.[35][39][40][41][42]

Furthermore, Siraj-ud-Daula believed that the British East India Company did not receive any permission from the Mughal Emperor Alamgir II to fortify their positions in the territories of the Nawab of Bengal.[43]

Conspiracy

The Nawab was infuriated on learning of the attack on Chandernagar. His former hatred of the British returned, but he now felt the need to strengthen himself by alliances against the British. The Nawab was plagued by fear of attack from the north by the Afghans under Ahmad Shah Durrani and from the west by the Marathas. Therefore, he could not deploy his entire force against the British for fear of being attacked from the flanks. A deep distrust set in between the British and the Nawab. As a result, Siraj started secret negotiations with Jean Law, chief of the French factory at Cossimbazar, and de Bussy. The Nawab also moved a large division of his army under Rai Durlabh to Plassey, on the island of Cossimbazar 30 miles (48 km) south of Murshidabad.[35][44][45][46]

Popular discontent against the Nawab flourished in his own court. The Seths, the traders of Bengal, were in perpetual fear for their wealth under the reign of Siraj, contrary to the situation under Alivardi's reign. They had engaged Yar Lutuf Khan to defend them in case they were threatened in any way.[47] William Watts, the Company representative at the court of Siraj, informed Clive about a conspiracy at the court to overthrow the ruler. The conspirators included Mir Jafar, paymaster of the army, Rai Durlabh, Yar Lutuf Khan and Omichund, a merchant and several officers in the army.[48] When communicated in this regard by Mir Jafar, Clive referred it to the select committee in Calcutta on 1 May. The committee passed a resolution in support of the alliance. A treaty was drawn between the British and Mir Jafar to raise him to the throne of the Nawab in return for support to the British in the field of battle and the bestowal of large sums of money upon them as compensation for the attack on Calcutta. On 2 May, Clive broke up his camp and sent half the troops to Calcutta and the other half to Chandernagar.[49][50][51][52]

Mir Jafar and the Seths desired that the confederacy between the British and himself be kept secret from Omichund, but when he found out about it, he threatened to betray the conspiracy if his share was not increased to three million rupees (£300,000). Hearing of this, Clive suggested an expedient to the Committee. He suggested that two treaties be drawn – the real one on white paper, containing no reference to Omichund and the other on red paper, containing Omichund's desired stipulation, to deceive him. The Members of the Committee signed on both treaties, but Admiral Watson signed only the real one and his signature had to be counterfeited on the fictitious one.[53] Both treaties and separate articles for donations to the army, navy squadron and committee were signed by Mir Jafar on 4 June.[54][55][56][57]

Clive testified and defended himself thus before the House of Commons of Parliament on 10 May 1773, during the Parliamentary inquiry into his conduct in India:

Omichund, his confidential servant, as *he* thought, told his master of an agreement made between the English and Monsieur Duprée [may be a mistranscription of Dupleix] to attack him, and received for that advice a sum of not less than four lacks of rupees. Finding this to be the man in whom the nabob entirely trusted, it soon became our object to consider him as a most material engine in the intended revolution. We therefore made such an agreement as was necessary for the purpose, and entered into a treaty with him to satisfy his demands. When all things were prepared, and the evening of the event was appointed, Omichund informed Mr. Watts, who was at the court of the nabob, that he insisted upon thirty lacks of rupees, and five per cent. upon all the treasure that should be found; that, unless that was immediately complied with, he would disclose the whole to the nabob; and that Mr. Watts, and the two other English gentlemen then at the court, should be cut off before the morning. Mr. Watts, immediately on this information, dispatched an express to me at the council. I did not hesitate to find out a stratagem to save the lives of these people, and secure success to the intended event. For this purpose we signed another treaty. The one was called the *Red*, the other the *White* treaty. This treaty was signed by every one, except admiral Watson; and I should have considered myself sufficiently authorised to put his name to it, by the conversation I had with him. As to the person who signed admiral Watson's name to the treaty, whether he did it in his presence or not, I cannot say; but this I know, that he thought he had sufficient authority for so doing. This treaty was immediately sent to Omichund, who did not suspect the stratagem. The event took place, and success attended it; and the House, I am fully persuaded, will agree with me, that, when the very existence of the Company was at stake, and the lives of these people so precariously situated, and so certain of being destroyed, it was a matter of true policy and of justice to deceive so great a villain.[58][59]

Approach march

Clive's solitary reflection before the Battle of Plassey

On 12 June, Clive was joined by Major Kilpatrick with the rest of the army from Calcutta at Chandernagar. The combined force consisted of 613 Europeans, 171 artillery-men controlling eight field pieces and two howitzers, 91 topasses, 2100 sepoys (mainly dusadhs)[60][61] and 150 sailors. The army set out for Murshidabad on 13 June. Clive sent out the Nawab's messengers with a letter declaring his intention to march his army to Murshidabad to refer their complaints with regard to the treaty of 9 February with the principal officers of the Nawab's government. The Indian troops marched on shore while the Europeans with the supplies and artillery were towed up the river in 200 boats. On 14 June, Clive sent a declaration of war to Siraj. On 15 June, after ordering an attack on Mir Jafar's palace in suspicion of his alliance with the British, Siraj obtained a promise from Mir Jafar to not join the British in the field of battle.[62] He then ordered his entire army to move to Plassey, but the troops refused to quit the city until the arrears of their pay were released. The delay caused the army to reach Plassey only by 21 June.[63][64][65][66]

By 16 June, the British force had reached Paltee, 12 miles (19 km) north of which lay the strategically important town and fort of Katwa. It contained large stores of grain and military supplies and was covered by the river Aji. On 17 June, Clive despatched a force of 200 Europeans, 500 sepoys, one field piece and a small howitzer under Major Coote of the 39th Foot to capture the fort. The detachment found the town abandoned when they landed at midnight. At daybreak on 19 June, Major Coote went to the bank of the river and waved a white flag, but was met only by shot and a show of defiance by the governor. Coote split his Anglo-Indian force; the sepoys crossed the river and fired the ramparts while the Europeans crossed farther up from the fort. When the garrison saw the advancing troops, they gave up their posts and fled north. Hearing of the success, Clive and the rest of the army arrived at Katwa by the evening of 19 June.[65][67][68]

At this juncture, Clive faced a dilemma. The Nawab had reconciled with Mir Jafar and had posted him on one flank of his army. Mir Jafar had sent messages to Clive, declaring his intention to uphold the treaty between them. Clive decided to refer the problem to his officers and held a council of war on 21 June. The question Clive put before them was whether, under the present circumstances, the army, without other assistance, should immediately cross into the island of Cossimbazar and attack the Nawab or whether they should fortify their position in Katwa and trust to assistance from the Marathas or other Indian powers. Of the twenty officers attending the council, thirteen including Clive were against immediate action, while the rest including Major Coote were in favour citing recent success and the high spirits of the troops. The council broke up and after an hour of deliberation, Clive gave the army orders to cross the Bhagirathi River (another name for the Hooghly River) on the morning of 22 June.[69][70][71][72][73]

At 1:00, on 23 June, they reached their destination beyond the village of Plassey. They quickly occupied the adjoining mango grove, called Laksha Bagh, which was 800 yards (730 m) long and 300 yards (270 m) wide and enclosed by a ditch and a mud wall. Its length was angled diagonally to the Bhagirathi River. A little to the north of the grove at the bank of the river stood a hunting lodge enclosed by a masonry wall where Clive took up his quarters. The grove was about a mile from the Nawab's entrenchments. The Nawab's army had been in place 26 hours before Clive's. A French detachment under Jean Law would reach Plassey in two days. Their army lay behind earthen entrenchments running at right angles to the river for 200 yards (180 m) and then turning to the north-eastern direction for 3 miles (4.8 km). There was a redoubt mounted by cannon at this turning along the entrenchment. There was a small hill covered by trees 300 yards (270 m) east of the redoubt. 800 yards (730 m) towards the British position was a small tank (reservoir) and 100 yards (91 m) further south was a larger tank, both surrounded by a large mound of earth.[74][75][76][77]

Order of battle

This section **does not** cite any sources. Please help improve this section by adding citations to reliable sources. Unsourced material may be challenged and removed. *(June 2018) (Learn how and when to remove this template message)*

The Anglo-Indian Army (East India Company)

Unit
Commander
Complement
Commander-in-Chief

Col. Robert Clive

1st Division (1st Madras European Regiment)
Maj. James Kilpatrick

2nd Division (1st Madras & Bombay European Regiments)
Maj. Alexander Grant

3rd Division (HM's 39th Regiment of Foot)
Maj. Eyre Coote

4th Division (Bombay European Regiment)
Maj. George Frederick Guah (or Guapp)

Sepoys (1st Bengal Native Infantry)
2100
Artillery (9 Battery, 12th Regiment, Royal Artillery)
Lt. Hater
Cpt. William Jennings
150 (100 artillerymen, 50 sailors)
6 field pieces
2 howitzers

The Bengal Army
Unit
Commander
Complement
Commander-in-Chief

Siraj-ud-daulah

Advanced Cavalry
Mir Madan
Mohan Lal
5,000 cavalry
7,000 infantry
Left Wing
Mir Jafar
15,000 cavalry
35,000 infantry

Centre
Yar Lutuf Khan

Right Wing
Rai Durlabh

Artillery
53 pieces (mostly 32, 24 and 18-pounders)
French Artillery
St. Frais
50 French artillerymen
6 field pieces

Battle

The Nawab's artillery on movable platform. A large stage, raised six feet from the ground, carrying besides the cannon, all the ammunition belonging to it, and the gunners themselves who managed the cannon, on the stage itself. These machines were drawn by 40 or 50 yoke of white oxen, of the largest size, bred in the country of Purnea; and behind each cannon walked an elephant, trained to assist at difficult tugs, by shoving with his forehead against the hinder part of the carriage.

At daybreak on 23 June, the Nawab's army emerged from their camp and started advancing towards the grove. Their army consisted of 30,000 infantry of all sorts, armed with matchlocks, swords, pikes and rockets and 20,000 cavalry, armed with swords or long spears, interspersed by 300 pieces of artillery, mostly 32, 24 and 18-pounders. The army also included a detachment of about 50 French artillerymen under de St. Frais directing their own field pieces. The French took up positions at the larger tank with four light pieces advanced by two larger pieces, within a mile of the grove. Behind them were a body of 5,000 cavalry and 7,000 infantry commanded by the Nawab's faithful general Mir madan Khan and Diwan Mohanlal. The rest of the army numbering 45,000 formed an arc from the small hill to a position 800 yards (730 m) east of the southern angle of the grove, threatening to surround Clive's relatively smaller army. The right arm of their army was commanded by Rai Durlabh, the centre by Yar Lutuf Khan and the left arm closest to the British by Mir Jafar.[78][79][80]

Clive watched the situation unfolding from the roof of the hunting lodge, anticipating news from Mir Jafar. He ordered his troops to advance from the grove and line up facing the larger tank. His army consisted of 750 European infantry with 100 Topasses, 2100 sepoys (dusadhs)[60] and 100 artillery-men assisted by 50 sailors. The artillery consisted of eight 6-pounders and two howitzers. The Europeans and Topasses were placed in the centre of the line in four divisions, flanked on both sides by three 6-pounders. The sepoys were placed on the right and left in equal divisions. Clive posted two 6-pounders and two howitzers behind some brick-kilns 200 yards (180 m) north of the left division of his army to oppose the French fire.[81][82][83]

Battle begins

At 8:00, the French artillery at the larger tank fired the first shot, killing one and wounding another from the grenadier company of the 39th Regiment. This, as a signal, the rest of the Nawab's artillery started a heavy and continuous fire. The advanced field pieces of the British opposed the French fire, while those with the battalion opposed the rest of the Nawab's artillery. Their shots did not serve to immobilize the artillery but hit the infantry and cavalry divisions. By 8:30, the British had lost 10 Europeans and 20 sepoys. Leaving the advanced artillery at the brick kilns, Clive ordered the army to retreat back to relative shelter of the grove. The rate of casualties of the British dropped substantially due to the protection of the embankment.[84][85][86]

Death of Mir Madan Khan

A soldier of the 39th Regiment of Foot stands with his rifle (c. 1742)

Soldier of the 39th Regiment of Foot (c. 1742)

At the end of three hours, there was no substantial progress and the positions of both sides had not changed. Clive called a meeting of his staff to discuss the way ahead. It was concluded that the present position would be maintained till after nightfall, and an attack on the Nawab's camp should be attempted at midnight. Soon after the conference, a heavy rainstorm occurred. The British used tarpaulins to protect their ammunition, while the Nawab's army took no such precautions. As a result, their gunpowder got drenched and their rate of fire slackened, while Clive's artillery kept up a continuous fire. As the rain began to subside, Mir Madan Khan, assuming that the British guns were rendered ineffective by the rain, led his cavalry to a charge. However, the British countered the charge with heavy grape shot, mortally wounding Mir Madan Khan and driving back his men.[87][88][89][90]

Siraj had remained in his tent throughout the cannonade surrounded by attendants and officers assuring him of victory. When he heard that Mir Madan was mortally wounded, he was deeply disturbed and attempted reconciliation with Mir Jafar, flinging his turban to the ground, entreating him to defend it. Mir Jafar promised his services but immediately sent word of this encounter to Clive, urging him to push forward. Following Mir Jafar's exit from the Nawab's tent, Rai Durlabh urged Siraj to withdraw his army behind the entrenchment and advised him to return to Murshidabad leaving the battle to his generals. Siraj complied with this advice and ordered the troops under Mohan Lal to retreat behind the entrenchment. He then mounted a camel and accompanied by 2,000 horsemen set out for Murshidabad.[91][92][93][94]

Battlefield manoeuvres

A plan depicting the positions and movements of the opposing armies in the Battle of Plassey

A plan of the Battle of Plassey, fought 23 June 1757 by Col. Robert Clive, against the Nawab of Bengal. Depiction of the battlefield, with explanations of troop movements.

At about 14:00, the Nawab's army ceased the cannonade and began turning back north to their entrenchments, leaving St. Frais and his artillery without support. Seeing the Nawab's forces retiring, Major Kilpatrick, who had been left in charge of the British force while Clive was resting in the hunting lodge, recognised the opportunity to cannonade the retiring enemy if St. Frais' position could be captured. Sending an officer to Clive to explain his actions, he took two companies of the 39th Regiment and two field pieces and advanced towards St. Frais' position. When Clive received the message, he hurried to the detachment and reprimanded Kilpatrick for his actions without orders and commanded to bring up the rest of the army from the grove. Clive himself then led the army against St. Frais' position which was taken at 15:00 when the French artillery retreated to the redoubt of the entrenchment, setting up for further action.[94][95][96][97]

9 (Plassey) Battery Royal Artillery of the British Military.

As the British force moved towards the larger tank, it was observed that the left arm of the Nawab's army had lingered behind the rest. When the rear of this division reached a point in a line with the northern point of the grove, it turned left and marched towards the grove. Clive, unaware that it was Mir Jafar's division, supposed that his baggage and stores were the intended target and sent three platoons under Captain Grant and Lieutenant Rumbold and a field piece under John Johnstone, a volunteer, to check their advance. The fire of the field piece halted the advance of the division, which remained isolated from the rest of the Nawab's army.[98][99][100]

English guns at The battle of Plassey, 23 June 1757

Meanwhile, the British field pieces began a cannonade on the Nawab's camp from the mound of the larger tank. As a result, many of the Nawab's troops and artillery started coming out of the entrenchment. Clive advanced half of his troops and artillery to the smaller tank and the other half to a rising ground 200 yards (180 m) to the left of it and started bombarding the entrenchment with greater efficiency, throwing the approaching trains into confusion. The Nawab's troops shot their matchlocks from holes, ditches, hollows and from bushes on the hill east of the redoubt while St. Frais kept up his artillery fire from the redoubt. Cavalry charges were also repulsed by the British field pieces. However, the British force sustained most of its casualties in this phase.[101][102][103]

At this point, Clive realised that the lingering division was Mir Jafar's and concentrated his efforts at capturing the redoubt and hill east of it. Clive ordered a three-pronged attack with simultaneous attacks by two detachments on the redoubt and the hill supported by the main force in the centre. Two companies of grenadiers of the 39th Regiment, under Major Coote took the hill at 16:30 after the enemy fled without firing a shot. Coote pursued them across the entrenchment. The redoubt was also taken after St. Frais was forced to retreat. By 17:00, the British occupied the entrenchment and the camp left by a dispersing army. The British troops marched on and halted 6 miles (9.7 km) beyond Daudpur at 20:00.[104][105][106]

The British losses were estimated at 22 killed and 50 wounded. Of the killed, three were of the Madras Artillery, one of the Madras Regiment and one of the Bengal European Regiment. Of the wounded, four were of the 39th Regiment, three of the Madras Regiment, four of the Madras Artillery, two of the Bengal European Regiment, one of the Bengal Artillery and one of the Bombay Regiment. Of the losses by the sepoys, four Madras and nine Bengal sepoys were killed while nineteen Madras and eleven Bengal sepoys were wounded. Clive estimates that the Nawab's force lost 500 men, including several key officers.[107]

Aftermath

In the evening of 23 June, Clive received a letter from Mir Jafar asking for a meeting with him. Clive replied that he would meet Mir Jafar at Daudpur the next morning. When Mir Jafar arrived at the British camp at Daudpur in the morning, Clive embraced him and saluted him as the Nawab of Bengal, Bihar and Odisha. He then advised Mir Jafar to hasten to Murshidabad to prevent Siraj's escape and the plunder of his treasure. Mir Jafar reached Murshidabad with his troops on the evening of 24 June. Clive arrived at Murshidabad on 29 June with a guard of 200 European soldiers and 300 sepoys in the wake of rumours of a possible attempt on his life. Clive was taken to the Nawab's palace, where he was received by Mir Jafar and his officers. Clive placed Mir Jafar on the throne and acknowledging his position as Nawab, presented him with a plate of gold rupees.[108][109]

Siraj-ud-daulah had reached Murshidabad at midnight on 23 June. He summoned a council where some advised him to surrender to the British, some to continue the war and some to prolong his flight. At 22:00 on 24 June, Siraj disguised himself and escaped northwards on a boat with his wife and valuable jewels. His intention was to escape to Patna with aid from Jean Law. At midnight on 24 June, Mir Jafar sent several parties in pursuit of Siraj. On 2 July, Siraj reached Rajmahal and took shelter in a deserted garden but was soon discovered and betrayed to the local military governor, the brother of Mir Jafar, by a man who was previously arrested and punished by Siraj. His fate could not be decided by a council headed by Mir Jafar and was handed over to Mir Jafar's son, Miran, who had Siraj murdered that night. His remains were paraded on the streets of Murshidabad the next morning and were buried at the tomb of Alivardi Khan.[110][111][112]

According to the treaty drawn between the British and Mir Jafar, the British acquired all the land within the Maratha Ditch and 600 yards (550 m) beyond it and the zamindari of all the land between Calcutta and the sea. Besides confirming the firman of 1717, the treaty also required the restitution, including donations to the navy squadron, army and committee, of 22,000,000 rupees (£2,750,000) to the British for their losses. However, since the wealth of Siraj-ud-daulah proved to be far less than expected, a council held with the Seths and Rai Durlabh on 29 June decided that one half of the amount was to be paid immediately – two-thirds in coin and one third in jewels and other valuables. As the council ended, it was revealed to Omichund that he would receive nothing with regard to the treaty, hearing which he went insane.[113][114]

Effects

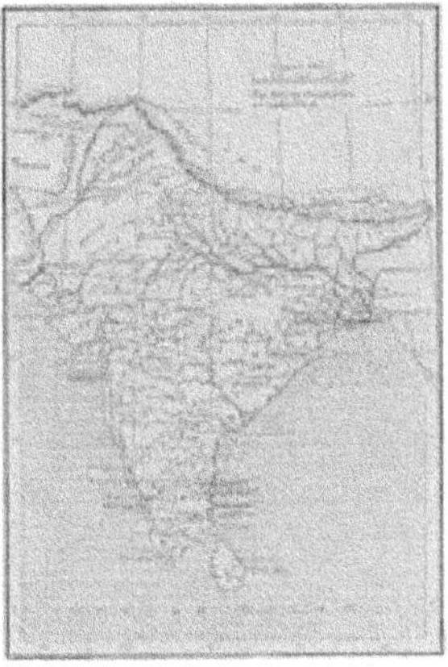

1744

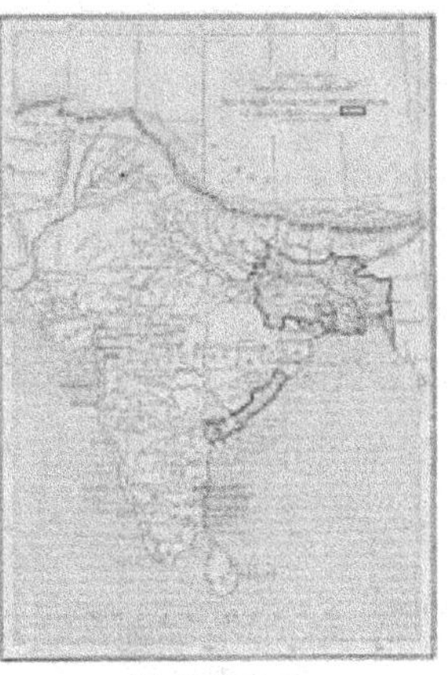

1767
British territorial possessions in India

Political effects

As a result of the war of Plassey, the French were no longer a significant force in Bengal. In 1759, the British defeated a larger French garrison at Masulipatam, securing the Northern Circars. By 1759, Mir Jafar felt that his position as a subordinate to the British could not be tolerated. He started encouraging the Dutch to advance against the British and eject them from Bengal. In late 1759, the Dutch sent seven large ships and 1400 men from Java to Bengal under the pretext of reinforcing their Bengal settlement of Chinsura even though Britain and Holland were not officially at war. Clive, however, initiated immediate offensive operations by land and sea and defeated the much larger Dutch force on 25 November 1759 in the Battle of Chinsura. The British then deposed Mir Jafar and installed Mir Qasim as the Nawab of Bengal. The British were now the paramount European power in Bengal. When Clive returned to England due to ill-health, he was rewarded with an Irish peerage, as Lord Clive, Baron of Plassey and also obtained a seat in the British House of Commons.[115][116]

The struggle continued in areas of the Deccan and Hyderabad such as <u>Arcot</u>, <u>Wandewash</u>, <u>Tanjore</u> and <u>Cuddalore</u>, culminating in 1761 when Col. Eyre Coote defeated a French garrison under de Lally, supported by <u>Hyder Ali</u> at <u>Pondicherry</u>. The French were returned Pondicherry in 1763 by way of the <u>Treaty of Paris</u> but they never again regained their former stature in India. The British would, in effect, emerge as rulers of the subcontinent in subsequent years.[117][118]

Economic effects[<u>edit</u>]

The Battle of Plassey and the resultant victory of the <u>British East India company</u> led to puppet governments instated by them in various states of India. This led to an unleashing of excesses, malpractices and atrocities by the British East India Company in the name of tax collection.[119]

The battlefield today

A monument was established in the battlefield, named the <u>Palashi Monument</u>.

Obelisks of Mirmadan, Nabe Singh Hajari & Bahadur Khan near Palashi battlefield

Plassey Monument in the battlefield

Mir Madan's Tomb, Faridpur, Murshidabad

CH 9 BATTLE OF PANIPAT

First Battle of Panipat

First Battle of Panipat

Part of <u>Mughal conquests</u>

The battle of Panipat and
the death of Sultan Ibrāhīm

Date
21 April 1526
Location
<u>Panipat</u>
(in present-day <u>Haryana</u>, India)

<u>29.39°N 76.97°E</u>

Result
Decisive Mughal victory
Sack of Delhi
End of the <u>Lodi dynasty</u>
Fall of the <u>Delhi Sultanate</u>
Establishment of the <u>Mughal Empire</u>

Territorial changes
<u>Delhi Sultanate</u> annexed by the Mughals

Belligerents

<u>Fictional flag of Timurids theDelhi Mughal Empire.svg</u>
<u>Lodi dynasty</u>

Commanders and leaders

<u>Fictional flag of the Mughal Empire.svg</u>
<u>Babur</u>

<u>Bhai Lalo</u>
<u>Fictional flag of the Mughal Empire.svg</u>

• 101 •

Ustad Timur Khan

Ustad Ali Quli

Mustafa Rumi

Malik Hast

Khosrau Sanghar Ali Khan

Ibrahim Lodi †

Hamid Khan †

Strength

12,000–12000 soldiers [2]

15-20 field guns[1]

100000 soldiers est.[2]

1000 elephants[3]

Casualties and losses

5000

20,000[4]

show

- v
- t
- e

Campaigns of Babur

The **First Battle of Panipat**, on 21 April 1526, was fought between the invading forces of Babur and the Lodi Kingdom. It took place in north India and marked the beginning of the Mughal Empire and the end of the Delhi Sultanate. This was one of the earliest battles involving gunpowder firearms and field artillery in the Indian subcontinent which were introduced by Mughals in this battle.[5]

The battle of Panipat between the armies of Babur and Ibrahim Lodi (1526). Babur was invited by Daulat Khan Lodi to enter India and defeat Ibrahim Lodi.[6] An illustration to the Vaqi 'at-i Baburi, by Deo Gujarati, c. 1590

Contents

- 1Background
- 2Battle

  - 2.1Advantage of cannons in the battle
  - 2.2Tactics

- 3Aftermath
- 4See also
- 5References
- 6Sources

Background

After losing Samarkand for the second time, Babur gave attention to conquer India as he reached the banks of the Chenab in 1519.[7] Until 1524, his aim was to only expand his rule to Punjab, mainly to fulfil his ancestor Timur's legacy, since it used to be part of his empire.[8] At that time, parts of north India were under the rule of Ibrahim Lodi of the Lodi dynasty, but the empire was crumbling and there were many defectors. He received invitations from Daulat Khan Lodi, Governor of Punjab and Ala-ud-Din, uncle of Ibrahim.[9] He sent an ambassador to Ibrahim, asking him to get punished by him and he is rightful to the throne of the country, however, the ambassador was detained at Lahore and released months later.[7]

Babur started for Lahore, Punjab, in 1524 but found that Daulat Khan Lodi had been driven out by forces sent by Ibrahim Lodi.[10] When Babur arrived at Lahore, the Lodi army marched out and was routed.[10] In response, Babur burned and punished the people of Lahore for two days, then marched to Dipalpur, placing Alam Khan, another rebel uncle of Lodi's, as governor. Alam Khan was quickly overthrown and fled to Kabul. In response, Babur supplied Alam Khan with troops who later joined up with Daulat Khan Lodi and together with about 30,000 troops, they besieged Ibrahim Lodi at Delhi.[11] He defeated them and drove Alam's army off, and Babur realised Lodi would not allow him to occupy the Punjab.[11]

Battle

Hearing of the size of Ibrahim's army, Babur secured his right flank against the city of Panipat, while digging a trench covered with tree branches to secure his left flanks. In the centre, he placed 700 carts tied together with ropes. Between every two carts, there were breastworks for his matchlock men. Babur also ensured there [12]

When Ibrahim's army arrived, he found the approach to Babur's army too narrow to attack. While Ibrahim redeployed his forces to allow for the narrower front, Babur quickly took advantage of the situation to flank (*tulghuma*) the Lodi army.[2] Many of Ibrahim's troops were unable to get into action, and fled when the battle turned against Ibrahim.[13] Faced with musket fire, cannon fire and cavalry attacks from all sides, Ibrahim Lodi fought and died with 6,000 of his remaining troops.[2]

Advantage of cannons in the battle

Babur's guns proved decisive in battle, firstly because Ibrahim lacked any field artillery, but also because the sound of the cannon frightened Ibrahim's elephants, causing them to trample his own men.[1]

Tactics

This section **does not** cite any sources. Please help improve this section by adding citations to reliable sources. Unsourced material may be challenged and removed. *(April 2014) (Learn how and when to remove this template message)*

Babur introduced field guns at Panipat, 1526

Tactics used by Babur were the *tulguhma* and the *araba*. *Tulguhma* meant dividing the whole army into various units, viz. the Left, the Right and the Centre. The Left and Right divisions were further subdivided into Forward and Rear divisions. Through this, a small army could be used to surround the enemy from all sides. The Centre Forward division was then provided with carts (*araba*) which were placed in rows facing the enemy and tied to each other with animal hide ropes. Behind them were placed cannons protected and supported by mantlets which could be used to easily manoeuvre the cannons. These two tactics made Babur's artillery lethal. The cannons could be fired without any fear of being hit, as they were shielded by the bullock carts held in place by hide ropes. The heavy cannons could also be easily traversed onto new targets, as they could be manoeuvred by the mantlets which were on wheels.

Aftermath

Ibrahim Lodi died on the field of battle along with 20,000 of his troops. The battle of Panipat was militarily a decisive victory for Timurids. Politically it gained Babur new lands, and initiated a new phase of his establishment of the long-lasting Mughal Empire in the heart of the Indian Subcontinent.[14]

Second Battle of Panipat

Second Battle of Panipat

The defeat of Hemu,
Akbarnama.jpg

The defeat of Hemu, a c. 1590s painting by Kankar of the Second Battle of Panipat taken from the Akbarnama.

Date
5 November 1556

Location
Panipat (in present-day Haryana, India)

29.39°N 76.97°E

Result
Mughal Empire victory

Belligerents

Mughal Empire
Hem Chandra Vikramaditya

Commanders and leaders

- Akbar
- Bairam Khan
- Ali Quli Khan Shaibani
- Sikandar Khan Uzbak
- Abdulla Khan Uzbak
- Husain Quli Khan
- Sayyed Mahmud Khan
- Shah Quli Mahram

- Hemu †
- Ramya
- Shadi Khan Kakkar †

Strength

10,000 cavalry

- 30,000 cavalry
- 500 war elephants[1]

Casualties and losses

minimal

5000 dead

The **Second Battle of Panipat** was fought on 5 November 1556, between the Hindu emperor of north India Hem Chandra Vikramaditya and forces of Akbar. Hemu had conquered the states of Delhi and Agra a few weeks earlier by defeating the Mughals led by Tardi Beg Khan at the Battle of Delhi and proclaimed himself Raja Vikramaditya at a coronation in Purana Quila in Delhi. Akbar and his guardian Bairam Khan who, after listening the news of losing Agra and Delhi, had marched to Panipat to reclaim the lost territories. The two armies clashed at Panipat not far from the site of the First Battle of Panipat of 1526.

Hem Chandra and his forces held the numerical superiority. However, Hemu was wounded by an arrow in the middle of the battle and fell unconscious. Seeing their leader going down, his army panicked and dispersed. Unconscious and almost dead Hemu was captured and subsequently beheaded by Akbar later on. The battle ended in a decisive victory for the Mughal king.

Contents

Background

c. 1910s portrayal of Hem Chandra Vikramaditya, the last Hindu Emperor of Delhi

Humayun, the successor of Babur, the founder of the Mughal Empire, had lost his inheritance when he was chased out of India by Sher Shah Suri who established the Sur Empire in 1540. Delhi and Agra fell into Sher Shah's hands, but he died soon after in 1545 at Kalinjar. He was succeeded by his younger son, Islam Shah Suri, who was a capable ruler. However, upon his death in 1553, the Sur Empire was caught up in a succession battle and was plagued by rebellion and the secession of provinces. Humayun made use of this discord to recapture what was lost and on 23 July 1555, the Mughals defeated Sikandar Shah Suri and finally regained control over Delhi and Agra.[2]

Islam Shah's rightful successor, his 12-year-old son, Firoz Khan, had been murdered by his maternal uncle, who had taken the throne as Adil Shah Suri. The new ruler was however, more interested in the pursuit of pleasure than in the affairs of his state. Those were largely left to Hem Chandra, an old Hindu associate of Sher Shah Suri from Rewari, who had risen from humble circumstances to become both Adil Shah's Chief Minister as well as the general of the Suri army.[3] He was in Bengal when Humayun died on 26 January 1556. The Mughal emperor's death provided an ideal opportunity to Hem Chandra to defeat the Mughals and reclaim lost territory.[4]

Hemu started a rapid march from Bengal and drove the Mughals out of Bayana, Etawah, Bharthana, Bidhuna, Lakhna, Sambhal, Kalpi, and Narnaul.[4] In Agra, the governor evacuated the city and fled without a fight upon hearing of Hemu's impending invasion.[5] In pursuit of the governor, Hemu reached Tughlaqabad, a village just outside Delhi where he ran into the forces of the Mughal governor of Delhi, Tardi Beg Khan, and defeated them in the Battle of Tughlaqabad.[4] He took possession of Delhi after a day's battle on 7 October 1556[5] and claimed royal status assuming the title of Vikramaditya (or *Bikramjit*).[6]

Prelude

On hearing the disastrous news from Tughlaqabad, Humayun's successor, the 13-year-old Akbar and his guardian Bairam Khan soon set off for Delhi. In a stroke of luck, Ali Quli Khan Shaibani (later *Khan-i-Zaman*), who had been sent ahead with 10,000-strong cavalry force, chanced upon Hemu's artillery which was being transported under a weak guard. He was easily able to capture the entire train of artillery from the Afghans who abandoned the guns and fled without making a stand. This would prove to be a costly loss for Hemu.[7][8]

On 5 November 1556, the Mughal army met Hemu's army at the historic battlefield of Panipat. Akbar and Bairam Khan stayed in the rear, eight miles from the battleground.[9]

Formation

The Mughal army was led by Ali Quli Khan Shaibani with his 10,000 cavalry in the centre with Sikandar Khan Uzbak on the right and Abdulla Khan Uzbak towards the left. The vanguard was led by Husain Quli Beg and Shah Quli Mahram and included Bairam Khan's detachment of Turks.[7]

Hemu's army was numerically superior counting among its ranks a 30,000-strong cavalry consisting of Afghan horsemen and an elephant contingent numbering 500. Each war elephant was protected by plate armour and mounted by musketeers and crossbowmen. Hemu led his army himself into battle, atop an elephant named *Hawai*.[10] His left was led by his sister's son, Ramya, and the right by Shadi Khan Kakkar. His army was an experienced and confident lot and Hemu had, by this time, been victorious in 22 battles from Bengal to Punjab. In this battle however, Hemu had no artillery.[12]

Battle

Two armies so collided
That they struck fire out of water;
You'd say the air was all crimsoned daggers,
Their steel had all become solid rubies.
> Abu'l-Fazl, Akbarnama[13]

Hemu began the attack himself and loosed his elephants among the right and left wings of the Mughals. Those soldiers who were able to escape the rampage, rather than retreating, chose to veer to the sides and attack the flanks of Hemu's cavalry, pelting them with their superior archery. The Mughal centre also advanced and took up a defensive position before a deep ravine. Neither Hemu's elephant nor his horse units were able to cross the chasm to reach their opponents and were vulnerable to the projectile weapons being fired from the other side. Meanwhile, the Mughal cavalry on their swift mounts had made inroads into the Afghan ranks from the flanks as well as the rear and began targeting the elephants, either slashing at the legs of the great beasts or taking out their riders. Hemu was forced to pull back his elephants and the Afghan attack relented.[14]

Seeing the Afghan attack slackening, Ali Quli Khan led his cavalry out, circling around and falling upon the Afghan centre from the rear. Hemu, monitoring the battlefield from his howdah atop Hawai, immediately hurried to counter this charge. Even after seeing Shadi Khan Kakkar and another of his able lieutenants, Bhagwan Das, go down, he continued to lead counterattacks against the Mughals, running down any who challenged his elephants. It was a desperately contested battle but the advantage seemed to have tilted in favour of Hemu.[15] Both the wings of the Mughal army had been driven back and Hemu moved his contingent of war elephants and cavalry forward to crush their centre. It was at this point that Hemu, possibly on the cusp of victory, was wounded when he was struck in the eye by a chance Mughal arrow and collapsed unconscious. Seeing him going down triggered a panic in his army which broke formation and fled.[16][17] The battle was lost; 5000 dead lay on the field of battle and many more were killed while fleeing.[9]

Aftermath

The elephant carrying the unconscious and almost dead Hemu was captured after several hours of finishing the war and led to the Mughal camp. Bairam Khan asked the 13-year-old Akbar to behead Hemu, but he refused to take the sword to a dead man. Akbar was persuaded to touch Hemu's head with his sword after which Bairam Khan executed him.[17] Hemu's head was sent to Kabul to be hanged outside Delhi Darwaja, while his body was gibbeted on a gate in Purana Quila, Delhi, where he had his coronation on 6 October.[16] Several supporters and relatives of Hem Chandra were beheaded and a minaret [17] was later erected. The painting of this minarette is one of the popular 56 paintings of Akbar's tenure in Akbarnama. A memorial for Hem Chandra was erected at the spot in Panipat where he was beheaded. It is now known as *Hemu's Samadhi Sthal*.[18][19]

With the passing of Hemu, Adil Shah's fortunes also took a turn for the worse. He was defeated and killed by <u>Khizr Khan</u>, son of <u>Muhammad Khan Sur</u> of Bengal, in April 1557.[17][20] The spoils from the battle at Panipat included 120 of Hemu's war elephants whose destructive rampages so impressed the Mughals that the animals soon became an integral part of their military strategies.[21]

CH 10 BATTLE OF BUXAR

Battle of Buxar

This article **needs additional citations for** <u>verification</u>. Please help <u>improve this article</u> by <u>adding citations to reliable sources</u>. Unsourced material may be challenged and removed.

Find sources: <u>"Battle of Buxar"</u> – <u>news</u> · <u>newspapers</u> · <u>books</u> · <u>scholar</u> · <u>JSTOR</u> *(February 2009)* (*<u>Learn how and when to remove this template message</u>*)

Battle of Buxar
Part of <u>Bengal War</u>

<u>Battle of Buxar -Crown and company- Arthur Edward Mainwaring pg.144.jpg</u>

Date
22 October 1764
Location
Near <u>Buxar</u>
Result
<u>English East India Company</u> victory

Belligerents

 <u>Mughal Empire</u>[1]

- <u>Multan Subah</u>
- <u>Durrani</u> and <u>Rohilla</u> Factions

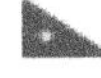 <u>English East India Company</u>

Commanders and leaders

<u>Shah Alam II</u>[1]

- <u>Amar Balach</u>
- <u>Mirza Najaf Khan</u>
- <u>Mir Qasim</u>
- <u>Shuja-ud-Daula</u>

Hector Munro of Novar

Strength

40,000
140 cannons
7,072
30 cannons

Casualties and losses

Disputed
British claim:[2]
2,000 killed
1,000 killed, wounded or missing[2][3]

show

- v
- t
- e

Seven Years' War
Bengal War

The **Battle of Buxar** was fought on 22 October 1764, between the forces under the command of the British East India Company, led by Hector Munro, and the combined armies of Mir Qasim, Nawab of Bengal till 1764; the Nawab of Awadh Shuja-ud-Daula; and the Mughal Emperor Shah Alam II.[4] The battle was fought at Buxar, a "small fortified town" within the territory of Bihar, located on the banks of the Ganga river about 130 kilometres (81 mi) west of Patna; it was a decisive victory for the British East India Company. The war was brought to an end by the Treaty of Allahabad in 1765.

Contents

- 1Battle
- 2Aftermath
- 3Gallery
- 4See also
- 5References
- 6External links

Battle

The British army engaged in the fighting numbered 7,072[5] comprising 859 British, 5,297 Indian sepoys and 918 Indian cavalry. The alliance army's numbers were estimated to be over 40,000. According to other sources[who?], the combined army of the Mughals, Awadh and Mir Qasim consisting of 40,000 men was defeated by a British army comprising 10,000 men. The Nawabs had virtually lost their military power after the battle of Buxar.

The lack of basic co-ordination among the three disparate allies was responsible for their decisive defeat.

Mirza Najaf Khan commanded the right flank of the Mughal imperial army and was the first to advance his forces against Major Hector Munro at daybreak; the British lines formed within twenty minutes and reversed the advance of the Mughals. According to the British, Durrani and Rohilla cavalry were also present and fought during the battle in various skirmishes. But by midday, the battle was over and Shuja-ud-Daula blew up large tumbrils and three massive magazines of gunpowder.

Munro divided his army into various columns and particularly pursued the Mughal Grand Vizier Shuja-ud-Daula the Nawab of Awadh, who responded by blowing up his boat-bridge after crossing the river, thus abandoning the Mughal Emperor Shah Alam II and members of his own regiment. Mir Qasim also fled with his 3 million rupees worth of Gemstones and later died in poverty in 1777. Mirza Najaf Khan reorganised formations around Shah Alam II, who retreated and then chose to negotiate with the victorious British.

Historian John William Fortescue claimed that the British casualties totalled 847: 39 killed and 64 wounded from the European regiments and 250 killed, 435 wounded and 85 missing from the East India Company's sepoys.[2] He also claimed that the three Indian allies suffered 2,000 dead and that many more were wounded.[2] Another source says that there were 69 European and 664 sepoy casualties on the British side and 6,000 casualties on the Mughal side.[3] The victors captured 133 pieces of artillery and over 1 million rupees of cash. Immediately after the battle Munro decided to assist the Marathas, who were described as a "warlike race", well known for their relentless and unwavering hatred towards the Mughal Empire and its Nawabs and Mysore.

Aftermath

The British victory at Buxar had "at one fell swoop", disposed of the three main scions of Mughal power in Upper India. Mir Kasim [Qasim] disappeared into an impoverished obscurity. Shah Alam realigned himself with the British, and Shah Shuja [Shuja-ud-Daula] fled west hotly pursued by the victors. The whole Ganges valley lay at the Company's mercy; Shah Shuja eventually surrendered; henceforth Company troops became the power-brokers throughout Oudh as well as Bihar".[6]

Gallery

The Mughal Emperor Shah Alam II, as a prisoner of the British East India Company, 1781

-

The Nawab of Bengal, Mir Qasim

- Shuja-ud-Daula served as the leading Nawab Vizier of the Mughal Empire, he was a lifelong of Shah Alam II.

Mirza Najaf Khan Baloch, the commander-in-chief of the Mughal Army.

Political map of the Indian Subcontinent in the year 1765.

Indo-Pakistani War of 1965

Indo–Pakistani War of 1965

Part of the Indo–Pakistani wars and conflicts
Kashmir region 2004.jpg

Geopolitical map of Kashmir provided by the United States CIA, c. 2004

Date
August – 23 September 1965
Location
Western Front

- Indo-Pakistani border

  ○ Line of Control, Working Boundary, Radcliffe Line, Sir Creek, and Zero-Point
  ○ Arabian sea

Eastern Front

- India-East Pakistan border

Result
Inconclusive

- United Nations mandated ceasefire.
- Both sides claim victory
- No permanent territorial changes (see Tashkent Declaration).

Belligerents

India

Pakistan

Commanders and leaders

India Sarvepalli Radhakrishnan
(President of India)

alt=India decoding=async class=thumbborder srcset="//upload.wikimedia.org/wikipedia/en/thumb/4/41/Flag_of_India.svg/35px-Flag_of_India.svg.png 1.5x, //upload.wikimedia.org/wikipedia/en/thumb/4/41/Flag_of_India.svg/45px-Flag_of_India.svg.png 2x" data-file-width=1350 data-file-height=900 v:shapes="_x0000_i1041"> Lal Bahadur Shastri
(Prime Minister of India)

decoding=async class=thumbborder srcset="//upload.wikimedia.org/wikipedia/commons/thumb/e/ea/Flag_of_Indian_Army.svg/35px-Flag_of_Indian_Army.svg.png 1.5x, //upload.wikimedia.org/wikipedia/commons/thumb/e/ea/Flag_of_Indian_Army.svg/46px-Flag_of_Indian_Army.svg.png 2x" data-file-width=900 data-file-height=450 v:shapes="_x0000_i1042"> Gen. J. N. Chaudhuri
(Chief of the Army Staff)

Lt. Gen. Harbaksh Singh
(GOC-in-C, Western Command)

Lt. Gen. P. O. Dunn
(GOC, I Corps)

Lt. Gen. Joginder Dhillon
(GOC, XI Corps)

Lt. Gen. Kashmir Katoch
(GOC, XV Corps)

AM Arjan Singh Aulakh
(Chief of the Air Staff)

Adm. Bhaskar Soman
(Chief of the Naval Staff)

Naval Ensign of Ayub Khan
(President of Pakistan)

Gen Musa Khan Hazara
(Cdr-in-Chief, Army)

Lt.Gen Bakhtiar Rana
(Commander, I Corps)

Lt.Gen Attiqur Rahman
(Commander, IV Corps)

MGen A.H. Malik
(GOC, 12th Infantry Division)

<u>MGen Yahya Khan</u>
(<u>GOC, 7th Infantry Division</u>)
<u>AM Nur Khan</u>
(<u>Cdr-in-Chief, Air Force</u>)
<u>VAdm A.R. Khan</u>
(<u>Cdr-in-Chief, Navy</u>)
<u>RAdm S.M. Ahsan</u>
((Cdr. <u>Eastern Naval Command</u>)
<u>Cdre S.M. Anwar</u>
(<u>OTC, 25th Destroyer Sqn</u>)

Strength

700,000 Infantry (Whole Army)[1]
700+ aircraft[2]
720 Tanks[1]

- 186 <u>Centurions</u>[3]
- 346 <u>Shermans</u>[1]
- 90 AMX[1][3]
- 90 <u>PT-76</u>[1]

628 Artillery[3]

- 66x 3.7"How[3]
- 450x <u>25pdr</u>[3]
- 96x 5.5"[3]
- 16x 7.2"[3]

Effective strength on the West Pakistan Border[4]

- 9 Infantry divisions (4 under-strength)
- 3 Armored brigades

260,000 Infantry (Whole Army)[1]
280 aircraft[2]
756 Tanks[3]

- 352 <u>Pattons</u>[3]
- 308 Shermans[3]
- 96 <u>Chaffees</u>[3]

552 Artillery[3]

- 72x105mm How[3]
- 234X25pdr[3]
- 126x155mm How[3]
- 48x8" How[3]
- 72x3.7" How[3]

- POK Lt Btys[3]

Effective strength on the West Pakistan Border[4]

- 6 Infantry divisions
- 2 Armored divisions

Casualties and losses

Neutral claims[5][6]

- 3,000 men[5]
- 150[7]–190 tanks[5]
- 60–75 aircraft[5]
- 540 km² (210 mi²) of territory lost (primarily in Kashmir)[8][9]

Indian claims

- 35[10]–59 aircraft lost[11] In addition, Indian sources claim that there were 13 IAF aircraft lost in accidents, and 3 Indian civilian aircraft shot down.[12]
- 520 km² (200 mi²) territory lost[13]

Pakistani claims

- 8,200 men killed or captured[13]
- 110[14]–113[13] aircraft destroyed
- 500 tanks captured or destroyed [13]
- 2602,[15] 2575 km²[13] territory gained
  1600 square miles territory gained according to Husain Haqqani

Neutral claims[5]

- 3,800 men[5]
- 200[5]-300 Tanks[16]
- 20 aircraft[5]
- Over 1,840 km² (710 mi²) of territory lost (in Sindh, Lahore, Sialkot, and Kashmir sectors)[8][9]

Pakistani claims

- 19 aircraft lost[14]

Indian claims

- 5259 men killed or captured [13]
- 43[17] –73 aircraft destroyed [13]
- 471 tanks destroyed [13]
- 1,735 km² (670 mi²) territory gained[13]

show

- <u>v</u>
- <u>t</u>
- <u>e</u>

Indo-Pakistani War of 1965

show

- <u>v</u>
- <u>t</u>
- <u>e</u>

Indo-Pakistani conflicts

The **Indo-Pakistani War of 1965** was a culmination of <u>skirmishes</u> that took place between April 1965 and September 1965 between <u>Pakistan</u> and <u>India</u>. The conflict began following Pakistan's <u>Operation Gibraltar</u>, which was designed to infiltrate forces into <u>Jammu and Kashmir</u> to precipitate an insurgency against Indian rule. India retaliated by launching a full-scale military attack on <u>West Pakistan</u>. The seventeen-day war caused thousands of casualties on both sides and witnessed the largest engagement of armored vehicles and the largest tank battle since World War II.[18][19] Hostilities between the two countries ended after a <u>United Nations</u>-mandated ceasefire was declared following diplomatic intervention by the Soviet Union and the United States, and the subsequent issuance of the <u>Tashkent Declaration</u>.[20] Much of the war was fought by the countries' land forces in <u>Kashmir</u> and along the <u>border</u> between India and Pakistan. This war saw the largest amassing of troops in Kashmir since the <u>Partition of India</u> in 1947, a number that was overshadowed only during the <u>2001–2002 military standoff</u> between India and Pakistan. Most of the battles were fought by opposing <u>infantry</u> and <u>armoured</u> units, with substantial backing from air forces, and naval operations. Many details of this war, like those of other <u>Indo-Pakistani Wars</u>, remain unclear.[21]

India had the <u>upper hand over Pakistan when the ceasefire was declared</u>.[22][23][24][25][26][27][28] Although the two countries fought to a standoff, the conflict is seen as a strategic and political defeat for Pakistan,[29][23][30][31][32][33][34] as it had neither succeeded in fomenting insurrection in Kashmir[35] nor had it been able to gain meaningful support at an international level.[30][36][37][38]

Internationally, the war was viewed in the context of the greater <u>Cold War</u>, and resulted in a significant geopolitical shift in the subcontinent.[39] Before the war, the United States and the United Kingdom had been major material allies of both India and Pakistan, as their primary suppliers of military hardware and foreign developmental aid. During and after the conflict, both India and Pakistan felt betrayed by the perceived lack of support by the western powers for their respective positions; those feelings of betrayal were increased with the imposition of an American and British embargo on military aid to the opposing sides.[39][40] As a consequence, India and Pakistan openly developed closer relationships with the Soviet Union and China, respectively.[40] The perceived negative stance of the western powers during the conflict, and during the 1971 war, has continued to affect relations between the West and the subcontinent. In spite of improved relations with the U.S. and Britain since the end of the Cold War, the conflict generated a deep distrust of both countries within the subcontinent which to an extent lingers to this day.[41][42][43]

Contents

Pre-war escalation

Since the Partition of British India in 1947, Pakistan and India remained in contention over several issues. Although the Kashmir conflict was the predominant issue dividing the nations, other border disputes existed, most notably over the Rann of Kutch, a barren region in the Indian state of Gujarat. The issue first arose in 1956 which ended with India regaining control over the disputed area.[44] Pakistani patrols began patrolling in territory controlled by India in January 1965, which was followed by attacks by both countries on each other's posts on 8 April 1965.[44][45] Initially involving border police from both nations, the disputed area soon witnessed intermittent skirmishes between the countries' armed forces. In June 1965, British Prime Minister Harold Wilson successfully persuaded both countries to end hostilities and set up a tribunal to resolve the dispute. The verdict, which came later in 1968, saw Pakistan awarded 350 square miles (910 km²) of the Rann of Kutch, as against its original claim of 3,500 square miles (9,100 km²).[46]

After its success in the Rann of Kutch, Pakistan, under the leadership of General Ayub Khan, believed the Indian Army would be unable to defend itself against a quick military campaign in the disputed territory of Kashmir as the Indian military had suffered a loss to China in 1962[21] in the Sino-Indian War. Pakistan believed that the population of Kashmir was generally discontented with Indian rule and that a resistance movement could be ignited by a few infiltrating saboteurs. Pakistan attempted to ignite the resistance movement by means of a covert infiltration, codenamed Operation Gibraltar.[47] The Pakistani infiltrators were soon discovered, however, their presence reported by local Kashmiris,[48] and the operation ended unsuccessfully.

The war

A declassified US State Department letter that confirms the existence of hundreds of "infiltrators" in the Indian-administered part of the disputed Kashmir region. Dated during the events running up to the 1965 war.

On 5 August 1965 between 26,000 and 33,000 Pakistani soldiers crossed the Line of Control dressed as Kashmiri locals headed for various areas within Kashmir. Indian forces, tipped off by the local populace, crossed the cease fire line on 15 August.[21]

Initially, the Indian Army met with considerable success, capturing three important mountain positions after a prolonged artillery barrage. By the end of August, however, both sides had relative progress; Pakistan had made progress in areas such as Tithwal, Uri and Poonch and India had captured the Haji Pir pass, 8 km into Pakistan administered Kashmir.[49]

On 1 September 1965, Pakistan launched a counterattack, called Operation Grand Slam, with the objective to capture the vital town of Akhnoor in Jammu, which would sever communications and cut off supply routes to Indian troops. Ayub Khan calculated that "Hindu morale would not stand more than a couple of hard blows at the right time and place"[50][51][52] although by this time Operation Gibraltar had failed and India had captured the Haji Pir Pass.[50][53] At 3:30 hours, on 1 September 1965, the entire Chhamb area came under massive artillery bombardment. Pakistan had launched operation Grand Slam and India's Army Headquarter was taken by surprise.[54] Attacking with an overwhelming ratio of troops and technically superior tanks, Pakistan made gains against Indian forces, who were caught unprepared and suffered heavy losses. India responded by calling in its air force to blunt the Pakistani attack. The next day, Pakistan retaliated, its air force attacked Indian forces and air bases in both Kashmir and Punjab. India's decision to open up the theatre of attack into Pakistani Punjab forced the Pakistani army to relocate troops engaged in the operation to defend Punjab. Operation Grand Slam therefore failed, as the Pakistan Army was unable to capture Akhnoor; it became one of the turning points in the war when India decided to relieve pressure on its troops in Kashmir by attacking Pakistan further south. In the valley, another area of strategic importance was Kargil. Kargil town was in Indian hands but Pakistan occupied high ground overlooking Kargil and Srinagar-Leh road. However, after the launch of a massive anti-infiltration operation by the Indian army, the Pakistani infiltrators were forced out of that area in the month of August.[55]

India crossed the International Border on the Western front on 6 September[56] On 6 September, the 15th Infantry Division of the Indian Army, under World War II veteran Major General Niranjan Prasad, battled a massive counterattack by Pakistan near the west bank of the Icchogil Canal (BRB Canal), which was a *de facto* border of India and Pakistan. The General's entourage itself was ambushed and he was forced to flee his vehicle. A second, this time successful, attempt to cross the Ichhogil Canal was made over the bridge in the village of Barki, just east of Lahore. These developments brought the Indian Army within the range of Lahore International Airport. As a result, the United States requested a temporary ceasefire to allow it to evacuate its citizens in Lahore. However, the Pakistani counterattack took Khem Karan from Indian forces which tried to divert the attention of Pakistanis from Khem Karan by an attack on Bedian and the adjacent villages.

The thrust against Lahore consisted of the 1st Infantry Division supported by the three tank regiments of the 2nd Independent Armoured Brigade; they quickly advanced across the border, reaching the Ichhogil (BRB) Canal by 6 September. The Pakistani Army held the bridges over the canal or blew up those it could not hold, effectively stalling any further advance by the Indians on Lahore. One unit of the Indian Jat Regiment, 3 Jat, had also crossed the Icchogil canal and captured[57] the town of Batapore (Jallo Mur to Pakistan) on the west side of the canal. The same day, a counter offensive consisting of an armoured division and infantry division supported by Pakistan Air Force Sabres forced the Indian 15th Division to withdraw to its starting point. Although 3 Jat suffered minimal casualties, the bulk of the damage being taken by ammunition and stores vehicles, the higher commanders had no information of 3 Jat's capture of Batapore and misleading information led to the command to withdraw from Batapore and Dograi to Ghosal-Dial. This move brought extreme disappointment[58] to Lt-Col Desmond Hayde, CO of 3 Jat. Dograi was eventually recaptured by 3 Jat on 21 September, for the second time but after a much harder battle due to Pakistani reinforcements.

On 8 September 1965, a company of 5 Maratha Light Infantry was sent to reinforce a Rajasthan Armed Constabulary (RAC) post at Munabao – a strategic hamlet about 250 kilometres from Jodhpur. Their brief was simple. To hold the post and to keep Pakistan's infantry battalions from overrunning the post at bay. But at Maratha Hill (in Munabao) – as the post has now been christened – the Indian company could barely manage to thwart the intense attack for 24 hours. A company of 3 Guards with 954 heavy mortar battery ordered to reinforce the RAC post at Munabao could never reach. The Pakistani Air Force had strafed the entire area, and also hit a railway train coming from Barmer with reinforcements near Gadra road railway station. On 10 September, Munabao fell into Pakistani hands, and efforts to capture the strategic point did not succeed.[59]

On the days following 9 September, both nations' premiere formations were routed in unequal battles. India's 1st Armoured Division, labeled the "pride of the Indian Army", launched an offensive towards Sialkot. The Division divided itself into two prongs, was forced back by the Pakistani 6th Armoured Division at Chawinda and was forced to withdraw after suffering heavy losses of nearly 100 tanks.

The Pakistanis followed up their success by launching Operation Windup, which forced the Indians back farther. Similarly, Pakistan's pride, the 1st Armoured Division, pushed an offensive towards Khem Karan, with the intent to capture Amritsar (a major city in Punjab, India) and the bridge on River Beas to Jalandhar.

The Pakistani 1st Armoured Division never made it past Khem Karan, however, and by the end of 10 September lay disintegrated by the defences of the Indian 4th Mountain Division at what is now known as the Battle of *Asal Uttar* (lit. meaning – "Real Answer", or more appropriate English equivalent – "Fitting Response"). The area became known as 'Patton Nagar' (Patton Town), because of the large number of US-made Pakistani Patton tanks. Approximately 97 Pakistani tanks were destroyed or abandoned, with only 32 Indian tanks destroyed or damaged. The Pakistani 1st Armoured Division less 5th Armoured Brigade was next sent to Sialkot sector behind Pakistan 6th Armoured Division where it didn't see action as 6th Armoured Division was already in process of routing Indian 1st Armoured Division which was superior to it in strength.

The hostilities in the Rajasthan sector commenced on 8 September. Initially Pakistan Desert Force and the Hur militia (followers of Pir Pagaro) was placed in a defensive role, a role for which they were well suited as it turned out. The Hurs were familiar with the terrain and the local area and possessed many essential desert survival skills which their opponents and their comrades in the Pakistan Army did not. Fighting as mainly light infantry, the Hur inflicted many casualties on the Indian forces as they entered Sindh. The Hurs were also employed as skirmishers, harassing the Indians LOC, a task they often undertook on camels. As the battle wore on the Hurs and the Desert Force were increasingly used to attack and capture Indian villages inside Rajasthan.[60]

The war was heading for a stalemate, with both nations holding territory of the other. The Indian army suffered 3,000 battlefield deaths, while Pakistan suffered 3,800. The Indian army was in possession of 758.9 miles² (1,920 km²) of Pakistani territory and the Pakistan army held 210 mile² (550 km²) of Indian territory.[61] The territory occupied by India was mainly in the fertile Sialkot, Lahore and Kashmir sectors,[62][63] while Pakistani ground gains were primarily in deserts opposite Sindh and in the Chumb sector near Kashmir.[63] Pakistan claims that it held 1600 square miles of Indian territory, while lost 450 square miles of its own territory.[64][65][66][67]

Aerial warfare

Main article: Indo-Pakistani Air War of 1965

Further information: Indian Air Force § Second Kashmir War 1965, and Pakistan Air Force § Indo-Pakistani War of 1965

Pakistani Sabre being shot down in combat by an Indian Gnat in September 1965 as seen from the Indian aircraft.

The war saw aircraft of the Indian Air Force (IAF) and the Pakistan Air Force (PAF) engaging in combat for the first time since independence. Although the two forces had previously faced off in the First Kashmir War during the late 1940s, that engagement was very limited in scale compared to the 1965 conflict.[citation needed]

The IAF was flying large numbers of Hawker Hunters, Indian-manufactured Folland Gnats, de Havilland Vampires, EE Canberra bombers and a squadron of MiG-21s. The PAF's fighter force comprised 102 F-86F Sabres and 12 F-104 Starfighters, along with 24 B-57 Canberra bombers. During the conflict, the PAF claimed it was out-numbered by around 5:1.[68]

The PAF's aircraft were largely of American origin, whereas the IAF flew an assortment of British and Soviet aeroplanes. It has been widely reported that the PAF's American aircraft were superior to those of the IAF.[citation needed]

The F-86 was vulnerable to the diminutive Folland Gnat, nicknamed "Sabre Slayer."[69] The Gnat is credited by many independent and Indian sources as having shot down seven Pakistani Canadair Sabres[a] in the 1965 war.[70][71] while two Gnats were downed by PAF fighters. The PAF's F-104 Starfighter of the PAF was the fastest fighter operating in the subcontinent at that time and was often referred to as "the pride of the PAF". However, according to Sajjad Haider, the F-104 did not deserve this reputation. Being "a high level interceptor designed to neutralise Soviet strategic bombers in altitudes above 40,000 feet," rather than engage in dogfights with agile fighters at low altitudes, it was "unsuited to the tactical environment of the region."[72] In combat the Starfighter was not as effective as the IAF's far more agile, albeit much slower, Folland Gnat fighter.[73][74] Yet it zoomed into an ongoing dogfight between Sabres and Gnats, at supersonic speed, successfully broke off the fight and caused the Gnats to egress. An IAF Gnat, piloted by Squadron Leader Brij Pal Singh Sikand, landed at an abandoned Pakistani airstrip at Pasrur, as he lacked the fuel to return to his base, and was captured by the Pakistan Army. According to the pilot, he got separated from his formation due to a malfunctioning compass and radio.[75][76] This Gnat is displayed as a war trophy in the Pakistan Air Force Museum, Karachi. Sqn Ldr Saad Hatmi who flew the captured aircraft to Sargodha, and later tested and evaluated its flight performance, was of view that Gnat was no "Sabre Slayer" when it came to dog fighting.[76] The Pakistan Air Force had fought well in countering the much large Indian Air Force and supported the ground forces.[77]

Captured Indian Folland Gnat on display at the PAF Museum Karachi.

The two countries have made contradictory claims of combat losses during the war and few neutral sources have verified the claims of either country. The PAF claimed it shot down 104 IAF planes and lost 19 of its own, while the IAF claimed it shot down 73 PAF planes and lost 59.[78] According to PAF, It flew 86 F-86 Sabres, 10 F-104 Starfighters and 20 B-57 Canberras in a parade soon after the war was over. Thus disproving the IAF's claim of downing 73 PAF fighters, which at the time constituted nearly the entire Pakistani front-line fighter force.[79] Indian sources have pointed out that, despite PAF claims of losing only a squadron of combat craft, Pakistan sought to acquire additional aircraft from Indonesia, Iraq, Iran, Turkey and China within 10 days of the beginning war.[citation needed]

The two air forces were rather equal in the conflict, because much of the Indian air force remained farther east to guard against the possibility of China entering the war.[80] According to the independent sources, the PAF lost some 20 aircraft while the Indians lost 60–75.[5][6] Pakistan ended the war having depleted 17 percent of its front line strength, while India's losses amounted to less than 10 percent.[citation needed] Moreover, the loss rate had begun to even out, and it has been estimated that another three week's fighting would have seen the Pakistani losses rising to 33 percent and India's losses totalling 15 percent.[citation needed] Air superiority was not achieved, and were unable to prevent IAF fighter bombers and reconnaissance Canberras from flying daylight missions over Pakistan. Thus 1965 was a stalemate in terms of the air war with neither side able to achieve complete air superiority.[80] However, according to Kenneth Werrell, the Pakistan Air Force "did well in the conflict and probably had the edge".[81] When hostilities broke out, the Pakistan Air Force with around 100 F-86s faced an enemy with five times as many combat aircraft; the Indians were also equipped with comparatively modern aircraft inventory. Despite this, Werrell credits the PAF as having the advantage of a "decade's experience with the Sabre" and pilots with long flight hours experience. One Pakistani fighter pilot, MM Alam, was credited with the record of downing five Indian aircraft in less than a minute, becoming the first known flying ace since the Korean War.[81] However, his claims were never confirmed by the PAF and is disputed by Indian sources[82][83][84] and some PAF officials.[85][86][87]

Tank battles

Main articles: Battle of Phillora, Battle of Asal Uttar, Battle of Burki, Lahore Front, and Battle of Chawinda

The 1965 war witnessed some of the largest tank battles since World War II. At the beginning of the war, the Pakistani Army had both a numerical advantage in tanks, as well as better equipment overall.[88] Pakistani armour was largely American-made; it consisted mainly of Patton M-47 and M-48 tanks, but also included many M4 Sherman tanks, some M24 Chaffee light tanks and M36 Jackson tank destroyers, equipped with 90 mm guns.[89] The bulk of India's tank fleet were older M4 Sherman tanks; some were up-gunned with the French high velocity CN 75 50 guns and could hold their own, whilst some older models were still equipped with the inferior 75 mm M3 L/40 gun. Besides the M4 tanks, India fielded the British-made Centurion Tank Mk 7, with the 105 mm Royal Ordnance L7 gun, and the AMX-13, PT-76, and M3 Stuart light tanks. Pakistan fielded a greater number and more modern artillery; its guns out-ranged those of the Indian artillery, according to Pakistan's Major General T.H. Malik.[90]

At the outbreak of war in 1965, Pakistan had about 15 armoured cavalry regiments, each with about 45 tanks in three squadrons. Besides the Pattons, there were about 200 M4 Shermans re-armed with 76 mm guns, 150 M24 Chaffee light tank and a few independent squadrons of M36B1 tank destroyers. Most of these regiments served in Pakistan's two armoured divisions, the 1st and 6th Armoured divisions – the latter being in the process of formation.

Destroyed Sherman Tank

The Indian Army of the time possessed 17 cavalry regiments, and in the 1950s had begun modernizing them by the acquisition of 164 AMX-13 light tanks and 188 Centurions. The remainder of the cavalry units were equipped with M4 Shermans and a small number of M3A3 Stuart light tanks. India had only a single armoured division, the 1st 'Black Elephant' Armoured Division, which consisted of the 17th Horse (The Poona Horse), also called 'Fakhr-i-Hind' ('Pride of India'), the 4th Horse (Hodson's Horse), the 16th Cavalry, the 7th Light Cavalry, the 2nd Lancers, the 18th Cavalry and the 62nd Cavalry, the two first named being equipped with Centurions. There was also the 2nd Independent Armoured Brigade, one of whose three regiments, the 3rd Cavalry, was also equipped with Centurions.

Despite the qualitative and numerical superiority of Pakistani armour,[91] Pakistan was outfought on the battlefield by India, which made progress into the Lahore-Sialkot sector, whilst halting Pakistan's counteroffensive on Amritsar;[92][93] they were sometimes employed in a faulty manner, such as charging prepared defences during the defeat of Pakistan's 1st Armoured Division at Asal Uttar.

After India breached the Madhupur canal on 11 September, the Khem Karan counter-offensive was halted, affecting Pakistan's strategy substantially.[50] Although India's tank formations experienced some results, India's attack at the Battle of Chawinda, led by its 1st Armoured Division and supporting units, was brought to halt by the newly raised 6th Armoured Division (ex-100th independent brigade group) in the Chawinda sector. Pakistan claimed that Indians lost 120 tanks at Chawinda,[94] compared to 44 of its own[95] But later, Indian official sources confirmed India lost only 29 tanks at Chawinda.[96][97] Neither the Indian nor Pakistani Army showed any great facility in the use of armoured formations in offensive operations, whether the Pakistani 1st Armoured Division at Asal Uttar or the Indian 1st Armoured Division at Chawinda. In contrast, both proved adept with smaller forces in a defensive role such as India's 2nd Armoured Brigade at Asal Uttar and Pakistan's 25th Cavalry at Chawinda.

The Centurion battle tank, with its 105 mm gun and heavy armour, performed better than the overly complex[need quotation to verify] Pattons.[93]

Naval hostilities

Naval operations did not play a prominent role in the war of 1965. On 7 September, a flotilla of the Pakistan Navy under the command of Commodore S.M. Anwar, carried out a bombardment of the Indian Navy's radar station coastal down of Dwarka, which was 200 miles (320 km) south of the Pakistani port of Karachi. Operation Dwarka, as it is known, is a significant naval operation of the 1965 war[98][99][100] contested as a nuisance raid by some.[101][102] The attack on Dwarka led to questions being asked in India's parliament[103] and subsequent post-war modernization and expansion of the Indian Navy, with an increase in budget from Rs. 35 crores to Rs. 115 crores.[104]

According to some Pakistani sources, one submarine, PNS *Ghazi*, kept the Indian Navy's aircraft carrier INS *Vikrant* besieged in Bombay throughout the war. Indian sources claim that it was not their intention to get into a naval conflict with Pakistan, and wished to restrict the war to a land-based conflict.[105] Moreover, they note that the Vikrant was in dry dock in the process of refitting. Some Pakistani defence writers have also discounted claims that the Indian Navy was bottled up in Bombay by a single submarine, instead stating that 75% of the Indian Navy was under maintenance in harbour.[106]

Covert operations

The Pakistan Army launched a number of covert operations to infiltrate and sabotage Indian airbases.[107] On 7 September 1965, the Special Services Group (SSG) commandos were parachuted into enemy territory. According to Commander-in-Chief of the Pakistan Army General Muhammad Musa, about 135 commandos were airdropped at three Indian airfields (Halwara, Pathankot and Adampur). The daring attempt proved to be an "unmitigated disaster".[107] Only 22 commandos returned to Pakistan as planned, 93 were taken prisoner (including one of the Commanders of the operations, Major Khalid Butt), and 20 were killed in encounters with the army, police or civilians.[citation needed] The reason for the failure of the commando mission is attributed to the failure to provide maps, proper briefings and adequate planning or preparation.[108]

Despite failing to sabotage the airfields, Pakistan sources claim that the commando mission affected some planned Indian operations. As the Indian 14th Infantry Division was diverted to hunt for paratroopers, the Pakistan Air Force found the road filled with transport, and destroyed many vehicles.[109]

India responded to the covert activity by announcing rewards for captured Pakistani spies or paratroopers.[110] Meanwhile, in Pakistan, rumors spread that India had retaliated with its own covert operations, sending commandos deep into Pakistan territory,[108] but these rumors were later determined to be unfounded.[111]

Assessment of losses

India and Pakistan make widely divergent claims about the damage they inflicted on each other and the amount of damage suffered by them. The following summarizes each nation's claims.

Indian claims[112]

Pakistani claims[113]

Independent Sources[21][114]

Casualties

- Army: 169 commissioned officers (1 brigadier, 9 lieutenant-colonels, 30 majors, 39 captains, 11 lieutenants, 79 second lieutenants), 80 junior commissioned officers (JCO), 1,820 other ranks[115][116][117][118][119][120][121][112]
- Air force: 19 officers, 21 other ranks[112]

—

3,000 Indian soldiers, 3,800 Pakistani soldiers

Combat flying effort

4,073+ combat sorties

2,279 combat sorties

Aircraft lost

59 IAF (official), 43 PAF.[111] In addition, Indian sources claim that there were 13 IAF aircraft lost in accidents, and 3 Indian civilian aircraft shot down.[12]

19 PAF, 104 IAF
20 PAF, 60–75 IAF; Pakistan claims India rejected neutral arbitration.[122][123]
Aerial victories
17 + 3 (post war)
30

–

Tanks destroyed
128 Indian tanks, 152 Pakistani tanks captured, 150 Pakistani tanks destroyed. Officially 471 Pakistani tanks destroyed and 38 captured[124]
165 Pakistan tanks[*dubious – discuss*][*citation needed*]
Land area won
1,500 sq mi (3,900 km^2) of Pakistani territory
250 sq mi (650 km^2) of Indian territory
India held 1,840 km^2 (710 sq mi) of Pakistani territory and Pakistan held 210 sq mi (540 km^2) of Indian territory

Neutral assessments

There have been several neutral assessments of the losses incurred by both India and Pakistan during the war. Most of these assessments agree that India had the upper hand over Pakistan when ceasefire was declared. Some of the neutral assessments are mentioned below —

- According to the Library of Congress Country Studies conducted by the Federal Research Division of the United States[24] –

The war was militarily inconclusive; each side held prisoners and some territory belonging to the other. Losses were relatively heavy—on the Pakistani side, twenty aircraft, 200 tanks, and 3,800 troops. Pakistan's army had been able to withstand Indian pressure, but a continuation of the fighting would only have led to further losses and ultimate defeat for Pakistan. Most Pakistanis, schooled in the belief of their own martial prowess, refused to accept the possibility of their country's military defeat by "Hindu India" and were, instead, quick to blame their failure to attain their military aims on what they considered to be the ineptitude of Ayub Khan and his government.

- Former *New York Times* reporter Arif Jamal wrote in his book *Shadow War*[9] —

This time, India's victory was nearly total: India accepted cease-fire only after it had occupied 740 square miles, though Pakistan had made marginal gains of 210 square miles of territory. Despite the obvious strength of the Indian wins, both countries claim to have been victorious.

- Devin T. Hagerty wrote in his book *South Asia in world politics*[125] –

The invading Indian forces outfought their Pakistani counterparts and halted their attack on the outskirts of Lahore, Pakistan's second-largest city. By the time United Nations intervened on September 22, Pakistan had suffered a clear defeat.

- In his book *National identity and geopolitical visions*,[126] Gertjan Dijkink writes –

The superior Indian forces, however, won a decisive victory and the army could have even marched on into Pakistani territory had external pressure not forced both combatants to cease their war efforts.

- An excerpt from Stanley Wolpert's *India*,[127] summarizing the Indo-Pakistani War of 1965,

In three weeks the second Indo-Pak War ended in what appeared to be a draw when the embargo placed by Washington on U.S. ammunition and replacements for both armies forced cessation of conflict before either side won a clear victory. India, however, was in a position to inflict grave damage to, if not capture, Pakistan's capital of the Punjab when the cease-fire was called, and controlled Kashmir's strategic Uri-Poonch bulge, much to Ayub's chagrin.

- In his book titled *The greater game: India's race with destiny and China*, David Van Praagh wrote[8] –

India won the war. It held on to the Vale of Kashmir, the prize Pakistan vainly sought. It gained 1,840 km² (710 sq mi) of Pakistani territory: 640 km² (250 sq mi) in Azad Kashmir, Pakistan's portion of the state; 460 km² (180 sq mi) of the Sailkot sector; 380 km² (150 sq mi) far to the south of Sindh; and most critical, 360 km² (140 sq mi) on the Lahore front. Pakistan took 540 km² (210 sq mi) of Indian territory: 490 km² (190 sq mi) in the Chhamb sector and 50 km² (19 sq mi) around Khem Karan.

- Dennis Kux's *India and the United States estranged democracies* also provides a summary of the war,[128]

Although both sides lost heavily in men and material, and neither gained a decisive military advantage, India had the better of the war. New Delhi achieved its basic goal of thwarting Pakistan's attempt to seize Kashmir by force. Pakistan gained nothing from a conflict which it had instigated.

- *A region in turmoil: South Asian conflicts since 1947* by Robert Johnson mentions[129] –

India's strategic aims were modest – it aimed to deny Pakistani Army victory, although it ended up in possession of 720 square miles (1,900 km²) of Pakistani territory for the loss of just 220 square miles (570 km²) of its own.

- An excerpt from William M. Carpenter and David G. Wiencek's *Asian security handbook: terrorism and the new security environment*[130] –

A brief but furious 1965 war with India began with a covert Pakistani thrust across the Kashmiri cease-fire line and ended up with the city of Lahore threatened with encirclement by Indian Army. Another UN-sponsored cease-fire left borders unchanged, but Pakistan's vulnerability had again been exposed.

- English historian John Keay's *India: A History* provides a summary of the 1965 war[131] –

The 1965 Indo-Pak war lasted barely a month. Pakistan made gains in the Rajasthan desert but its main push against India's Jammu-Srinagar road link was repulsed and Indian tanks advanced to within a sight of Lahore. Both sides claimed victory but India had most to celebrate.

- Uk Heo and Shale Asher Horowitz write in their book *Conflict in Asia: Korea, China-Taiwan, and India-Pakistan*[132] –

Again India appeared, logistically at least, to be in a superior position but neither side was able to mobilize enough strength to gain a decisive victory.

- According to the Office of the Historian within the U.S Department of State:[133]

Conflict resumed again in early 1965, when Pakistani and Indian forces clashed over disputed territory along the border between the two nations. Hostilities intensified that August when the Pakistani army attempted to take Kashmir by force. The attempt to seize the state was unsuccessful, and the second India-Pakistan War reached a stalemate.

Ceasefire

The United States and the Soviet Union used significant diplomatic tools to prevent any further escalation in the conflict between the two South Asian nations. The Soviet Union, led by Premier Alexei Kosygin, hosted ceasefire negotiations in Tashkent (now in Uzbekistan), where Indian Prime Minister Lal Bahadur Shastri and Pakistani President Ayub Khan signed the Tashkent Agreement, agreeing to withdraw to pre-August lines no later than 25 February 1966.

With declining stockpiles of ammunition, Pakistani leaders feared the war tilting in India's favor. Therefore, they quickly accepted the ceasefire in Tashkent.[134] Despite strong opposition from Indian military leaders, India bowed to growing international diplomatic pressure and accepted the ceasefire.[134] On 22 September, the United Nations Security Council unanimously passed a resolution that called for an unconditional ceasefire from both nations. The war ended the following day.

India's Prime Minister, Shastri, suffered a fatal heart attack soon after the declaration of the ceasefire. As a consequence, the public outcry in India against the ceasefire declaration transformed into a wave of sympathy for the ruling Indian National Congress.[135]

India and Pakistan accused each other of ceasefire violations; India charged Pakistan with 585 violations in 34 days, while Pakistan countered with accusations of 450 incidents by India.[136] In addition to the expected exchange of small arms and artillery fire, India reported that Pakistan utilized the ceasefire to capture the Indian village of Chananwalla in the Fazilka sector. This village was recaptured by Indian troops on 25 December. On 10 October, a B-57 Canberra on loan to the PAF was damaged by 3 SA-2 missiles fired from the IAF base at Ambala.[137] A Pakistani Army Auster AOP was shot down on 16 December, killing one Pakistani army captain; on 2 February 1967, an AOP was shot down by IAF Hunters.

The ceasefire remained in effect until the start of the Indo-Pakistani War of 1971.

Public perceptions

The ceasefire was criticised by many Pakistanis who, relying on fabricated official reports and the controlled Pakistani press, believed that the leadership had surrendered military gains. The protests led to student riots.[138] Pakistan State's reports had suggested that their military was performing admirably in the war – which they incorrectly blamed as being initiated by India – and thus the Tashkent Declaration was seen as having forfeited the gains.[139] Some recent books written by Pakistani authors, including one by ex-ISI chief Lieutenant General Mahmud Ahmed Durrani initially titled *The Myth of 1965 Victory*,[140] reportedly exposed Pakistani fabrications about the war, but all copies of the book were bought by Pakistan Army to prevent circulation because the topic was "too sensitive".[141][142] The book was published with the revised title *History of Indo Pak War 1965*, published by Services Book Club, a part of the Pakistan military and printed by Oxford University Press, Karachi. A few copies of the book have survived.[143] A version was published in India as *Illusion of Victory: A Military History of the Indo-Pak War-1965* by Lexicon Publishers.[144] Recently a new Pakistani impression has been published in 2017.

Intelligence failures

Strategic miscalculations by both India and Pakistan ensured that the war ended in a stalemate.

Indian miscalculations

Indian military intelligence gave no warning of the impending Pakistan invasion. The Indian Army failed to recognize the presence of heavy Pakistani artillery and armaments in Chumb and suffered significant losses as a result.

The "Official War History – 1965", drafted by the Ministry of Defence of India in 1992, was a long suppressed document that revealed other miscalculations. According to the document, on 22 September when the Security Council was pressing for a ceasefire, the Indian Prime Minister asked commanding Gen. Chaudhuri if India could possibly win the war, were he to delay accepting the ceasefire. The general replied that most of India's frontline ammunition had been used up and the Indian Army had suffered considerable tank losses. It was determined later that only 14% of India's frontline ammunition had been fired and India held twice the number of tanks as Pakistan. By this time, the Pakistani Army had used close to 80% of its ammunition.

Air Chief Marshal (retd) P.C. Lal, who was the Vice Chief of Air Staff during the conflict, points to the lack of coordination between the IAF and the Indian army. Neither side revealed its battle plans to the other. The battle plans drafted by the Ministry of Defence and General Chaudhari, did not specify a role for the Indian Air Force in the order of battle. This attitude of Gen. Chaudhari was referred to by ACM Lal as the "Supremo Syndrome", a patronizing attitude sometimes held by the Indian army towards the other branches of the Indian Military.[112]

Pakistani miscalculations

The Pakistani Army's failures started with the supposition that a generally discontented Kashmiri people, given the opportunity provided by the Pakistani advance, would revolt against their Indian rulers, bringing about a swift and decisive surrender of Kashmir. The Kashmiri people, however, did not revolt. Instead, the Indian Army was provided with enough information to learn of Operation Gibraltar and the fact that the Army was battling not insurgents, as they had initially supposed, but Pakistani Army regulars.

Telegram from the Embassy of the United States in Karachi: "Continuing propaganda regarding achievements of Pak forces seems to have convinced most that only Pak forbearance saved the Indians from disaster."

The Pakistani Army also failed to recognize that the Indian policy makers would order an attack on the southern sector in order to open a second front. Pakistan was forced to dedicate troops to the southern sector to protect Sialkot and Lahore instead using them to support penetrating into Kashmir.

"Operation Grand Slam", which was launched by Pakistan to capture Akhnoor, a town north-east of Jammu and a key region for communications between Kashmir and the rest of India, was also a failure. Many Pakistani commentators criticised the Ayub Khan administration for being indecisive during Operation Grand Slam. These critics claim that the operation failed because Ayub Khan knew the importance of Akhnoor to India (having called it India's "jugular vein") and did not want to capture it and drive the two nations into an all-out war. Despite progress being made in Akhnoor, General Ayub Khan relieved the commanding Major General Akhtar Hussain Malik and replaced him with Gen. Yahya Khan. A 24-hour lull ensued the replacement, which allowed the Indian army to regroup in Akhnoor and successfully oppose a lackluster attack headed by General Yahya Khan. "The enemy came to our rescue", asserted the Indian Chief of Staff of the Western Command. Later, Akhtar Hussain Malik criticised Ayub Khan for planning Operation Gibraltar, which was doomed to fail, and for relieving him of his command at a crucial moment in the war. Malik threatened to expose the truth about the war and the army's failure, but later dropped the idea for fear of being banned.[145]

Some authors have noted that Pakistan might have been emboldened by a war game – conducted in March 1965, at the Institute for Defense Analyses in the United States. The exercise concluded that, in the event of a war with India, Pakistan would win.[146][147] Other authors like Stephen P. Cohen, have consistently commented that the Pakistan Army had "acquired an exaggerated view of the weakness of both India and the Indian military ... the 1965 war was a shock".[148]

Pakistani Air Marshal and Commander-in-Chief of PAF during the war, Nur Khan, later said that the Pakistan Army, and not India, should be blamed for starting the war.[149][150] However propaganda in Pakistan about the war continued; the war was not rationally analysed in Pakistan,[151][152] with most of the blame being heaped on the leadership and little importance given to intelligence failures that persisted until the debacle of the Indo-Pakistani War of 1971.

Involvement of other nations

The United States and the United Kingdom had been the principal suppliers of military matériél to India and Pakistan since 1947. Both India and Pakistan were Commonwealth republics. While India had pursued a policy of nominal non-alignment, Pakistan was a member of both CENTO and SEATO and a purported ally of the West in its struggle against Communism.[153] Well before the conflict began, however, Britain and the United States had suspected Pakistan of joining both alliances out of opportunism to acquire advanced weapons for a war against India. They had therefore limited their military aid to Pakistan to maintain the existing balance of power in the subcontinent.[154] In 1959, however, Pakistan and the United States had signed an Agreement of Cooperation under which the United States agreed to take "appropriate action, including the use of armed forces" in order to assist the Government of Pakistan at its request.[155] By 1965, American and British analysts had recognised the two international groupings, CENTO and SEATO, and Pakistan's continued alliance with the West as being largely meaningless.[156]

Following the start of the 1965 war, both the United States and Britain took the view that the conflict was largely Pakistan's fault, and suspended all arms shipments to both India and Pakistan.[24] While the United States maintained a neutral stance, the British Prime Minister, Harold Wilson, condemned India for aggression after its army advanced towards Lahore; his statement was met with a furious rebuttal from India.[157]

Internationally, the level of support which Pakistan received was limited at best.[36][158][159] Iran and Turkey issued a joint communiqué on 10 September which placed the blame on India, backed the United Nations' appeal for a cease-fire and offered to deploy troops for a UN peacekeeping mission in Kashmir.[160] Pakistan received support from Indonesia, Iran, Turkey, and Saudi Arabia in the form of six naval vessels, jet fuel, guns and ammunition and financial support, respectively.[161]

Since before the war, the People's Republic of China had been a major military associate of Pakistan and a military opponent of India, with whom it had fought a brief war in 1962. China had also become a foreign patron for Pakistan and had given Pakistan $60 million in development assistance in 1965.[162] During the war, China openly supported the Pakistani position. It took advantage of the conflict to issue a strongly worded ultimatum to India condemning its "aggression" in Tibet and hinting at nuclear retaliation by China (China had exploded its first nuclear device the previous year).[159] Despite strong fears of Chinese intervention on the side of Pakistan, the Chinese government ultimately exercised restraint.[163] This was partly due to the logistical difficulties of a direct Chinese military intervention against India and India's improved military strength after its defeat by China in 1962.[158] China had also received strong warnings by the American and Soviet governments against expanding the scope of the conflict by intervening.[159] In the face of this pressure, China backed down, extending the deadline for India to respond to its ultimatum and warning India against attacking East Pakistan.[38] Ultimately, Pakistan rejected Chinese offers of military aid, recognising that accepting it would only result in further alienating Pakistan internationally.[159] International opinion considered China's actions to be dangerously reckless and aggressive, and it was soundly rebuked in the world press for its unnecessarily provocative stance during the conflict.[159]

India's participation in the Non-Aligned Movement yielded little support from its members.[164] Support given by Indonesia to Pakistan was seen as a major Indian diplomatic failure, as Indonesia had been among the founding members of the Non-Aligned Movement along with India.[citation needed] Despite its close relations with India, the Soviet Union was more neutral than other nations during the war, inviting both nations to peace talks under its aegis in Tashkent.[165][need quotation to verify]

Aftermath

India

Despite the declaration of a ceasefire, India was perceived as the victor due to its success in halting the Pakistan-backed insurgency in Kashmir.[31] In its October 1965 issue, the TIME magazine quoted a Western official assessing the consequences of the war[166] —

Now it's apparent to everybody that India is going to emerge as an Asian power in its own right.

In light of the failures of the Sino-Indian War, the outcome of the 1965 war was viewed as a "politico-strategic" victory in India. The Indian premier, Lal Bahadur Shastri, was hailed as a national hero in India.[167]

While the overall performance of the Indian military was praised, military leaders were criticised for their failure to effectively deploy India's superior armed forces so as to achieve a decisive victory over Pakistan.[168] In his book *War in the modern world since 1815*, noted war historian Jeremy Black said that though Pakistan "lost heavily" during the 1965 war, India's hasty decision to call for negotiations prevented further considerable damage to the Pakistan Armed Forces. He elaborates[169] —

India's chief of army staff urged negotiations on the ground that they were running out ammunition and their number of tanks had become seriously depleted. In fact, the army had used less than 15% of its ammunition compared to Pakistan, which had consumed closer to 80 percent and India had double the number of serviceable tanks.

In 2015, Marshal of the Indian Air Force Arjan Singh, the last surviving armed force commander of the conflict, gave his assessment that the war ended in a stalemate, but only due to international pressure for a ceasefire, and that India would have achieved a decisive victory had hostilities continued for a few days more:[170]

For political reasons, Pakistan claims victory in the 1965 war. In my opinion, the war ended in a kind of stalemate. We were in a position of strength. Had the war continued for a few more days, we would have gained a decisive victory. I advised then prime minister Lal Bahadur Shastri not to agree for ceasefire. But I think he was under pressure from the United Nations and some countries.

As a consequence, India focussed on enhancing communication and coordination within and among the tri-services of the Indian Armed Forces. Partly as a result of the inefficient information gathering preceding the war, India established the Research and Analysis Wing for external espionage and intelligence. Major improvements were also made in command and control to address various shortcomings and the positive impact of these changes was clearly visible during the Indo-Pakistani War of 1971 when India achieved a decisive victory over Pakistan within two weeks.

China's repeated threats to intervene in the conflict in support of Pakistan increased pressure on the government to take an immediate decision to develop nuclear weapons.[171] Despite repeated assurances, the United States did little to prevent extensive use of American arms by Pakistani forces during the conflict, thus irking India.[172] At the same time, the United States and United Kingdom refused to supply India with sophisticated weaponry which further strained the relations between the West and India.[173] These developments led to a significant change in India's foreign policy – India, which had previously championed the cause of non-alignment, distanced itself further from Western powers and developed close relations with the Soviet Union. By the end of the 1960s, the Soviet Union emerged as the biggest supplier of military hardware to India.[174] From 1967 to 1977, 81% of India's arms imports were from the Soviet Union.[175] After the 1965 war, the arms race between India and Pakistan became even more asymmetric and India was outdistancing Pakistan by far.[176]

Pakistan

At the conclusion of the war, many Pakistanis considered the performance of their military to be positive. 6 September is celebrated as Defence Day in Pakistan, in commemoration of the successful defence of Lahore against the Indian army. The performance of the Pakistani Air Force, in particular, was praised.

However, the Pakistani government was accused by analysts of spreading disinformation among its citizens regarding the actual consequences of the war.[177] In his book *Mainsprings of Indian and Pakistani foreign policies*, S.M. Burke writes[125] —

After the Indo-Pakistani war of 1965 the balance of military power had decisively shifted in favor of India. Pakistan had found it difficult to replace the heavy equipment lost during that conflict while her adversary, despite her economic and political problems, had been determinedly building up her strength.

Pakistani commentator Haidar Imtiaz remarked:[178]

The myth of 'victory' was created after the war had ended, in order to counter Indian claims of victory on the one hand and to shield the Ayub regime and the army from criticism on the other.

A book titled *Indo-Pakistan War of 1965: A Flashback*,[179] produced by the Inter-Services Public Relations of Pakistan, is used as the official history of the war, which omits any mention of the operations Gibraltar and Grand Slam, and begins with the Indian counter-offensive on the Lahore front. The Pakistan Army is claimed to have put up a "valiant defense of the motherland" and forced the attack in its tracks.[178]

Most observers agree that the myth of a mobile, hard hitting Pakistan Army was badly dented in the war, as critical breakthroughs were not made.[180] Several Pakistani writers criticised the military's ill-founded belief that their "martial race" of soldiers could defeat "Hindu India" in the war.[181][182] Rasul Bux Rais, a Pakistani political analyst wrote[183] —

The 1965 war with India proved that Pakistan could neither break the formidable Indian defences in a blitzkrieg fashion nor could she sustain an all-out conflict for long.

Historian Akbar S Zaidi notes that Pakistan "lost terribly in the 1965 war".[184]

The Pakistan airforce on the other hand gained a lot of credibility and reliability among Pakistan military and international war writers for successful defence of Lahore and other important areas of Pakistan and heavy retaliation to India on the next day. The alertness of the airforce was also related to the fact that some pilots were scrambled 6 times in less than an hour on indication of Indian air raids. The Pakistan airforce along with the army is celebrated on Defence day and Airforce day in commemoration of this in Pakistan (6 and 7 September respectively).[185][186]

Moreover, Pakistan had lost more ground than it had gained during the war and, more importantly, failed to achieve its goal of capturing Kashmir; this result has been viewed by many impartial observers as a defeat for Pakistan.[32][33][34]

Many senior Pakistani officials and military experts later criticised the faulty planning of Operation Gibraltar, which ultimately led to the war. The Tashkent declaration was also criticised in Pakistan, though few citizens realised the gravity of the situation that existed at the end of the war. Political leaders were also criticised. Following the advice of <u>Zulfikar Ali Bhutto</u>, Pakistan's foreign minister, Ayub Khan had raised very high expectations among the people of Pakistan about the superiority – if not invincibility – of its armed forces,[187] but Pakistan's inability to attain its military aims during the war created a political liability for Ayub.[188] The defeat of its Kashmiri ambitions in the war led to the army's invincibility being challenged by an increasingly vocal opposition.[189]

One of the farthest reaching consequences of the war was the wide-scale economic slowdown in Pakistan.[190][191] The war ended the impressive economic growth Pakistan had experienced since the early 1960s. Between 1964 and 1966, Pakistan's defence spending rose from 4.82% to 9.86% of GDP, putting a tremendous strain on Pakistan's economy. By 1970–71, defence spending comprised a whopping 55.66% of government expenditure.[192] According to veterans of the war, the war greatly cost Pakistan economically, politically, and militarily.[193] Nuclear theorist Feroze Khan maintained that the 1965 war was a last <u>conventional attempt</u> to snatch Kashmir by military force, and Pakistan's own position in the international community, especially with the <u>United States</u>, began to deteriorate from the point the war started, while on the other hand, the alliance with China saw improvements.[193] <u>Chairman joint chiefs</u> General <u>Tariq Majid</u> claims in his memoirs that <u>Chou En-Lai</u> had longed advised the government in the classic style of <u>Sun Tzu</u>: "to go slow, not to push India hard; and avoid a fight over Kashmir, 'for at least, 20–30 years, until you have developed your economy and consolidated your national power'."[193] General Majid maintained in *Eating Grass* that the "sane, philosophical and political critical thinking" was missing in Pakistan, and that the country had lost extensive human resources by fighting the war.[193]

Pakistan was surprised by the lack of support from the United States, an ally with whom the country had signed an Agreement of Cooperation. The US turned neutral in the war when it cut off military supplies to Pakistan (and India);[21] an action that the Pakistanis took as a sign of betrayal.[194] After the war, Pakistan would increasingly look towards China as a major source of military hardware and political support.

Another negative consequence of the war was growing resentment against the Pakistani government in <u>East Pakistan</u> (present day <u>Bangladesh</u>),[148] particularly for West Pakistan's obsession with Kashmir.[195] <u>Bengali</u> leaders accused the central government of not providing adequate security for East Pakistan during the conflict, even though large sums of money were taken from the east to finance the war for Kashmir.[196] In fact, despite some Pakistan Air Force attacks being launched from bases in East Pakistan during the war, India did not retaliate in that sector,[197] although East Pakistan was defended only by an understrengthed infantry division (14th Division), sixteen planes and no tanks.[198] <u>Sheikh Mujibur Rahman</u> was critical of the disparity in military resources deployed in East and West Pakistan, calling for greater autonomy for East Pakistan, an action that ultimately led to the <u>Bangladesh Liberation War</u> and <u>another war</u> between India and Pakistan in 1971.

Pakistan celebrates "Defence Day" every year to commemorate 6 September 1965 to pay tribute to the soldiers killed in the war.[199] However, Pakistani journalists, including Taha Siddiqui [200] and Haseeb Asif [201] have criticized the celebration of Defence Day.

Awards

National awards

- <u>Joginder Singh Dhillon</u>, Lt. Gen, awarded the <u>Padma Bhushan</u> in 1966 by the Government of India for his role in the 1965 war,[202] becoming the first Indian Army officer to receive the award.[203]

Gallantry awards

For bravery, the following soldiers were awarded the highest gallantry award of their respective countries, the Indian award <u>Param Vir Chakra</u> and the Pakistani award <u>Nishan-e-Haider</u>:

India

- Company Quarter Master Havildar Abdul Hamid[204] (Posthumous)
- Lieutenant-Colonel Ardeshir Burzorji Tarapore[204] (Posthumous)

Pakistan

- Major Raja Aziz Bhatti Shaheed[205] (Posthumous)

Battle honours

After the war, a total of 16 battle honours and 3 theatre honours were awarded to units of the Indian Army, the notable amongst which are:[206]

Indian Prime Minister Narendra Modi and other politicians visit Shauryanjali, a commemorative exhibition on the 1965 war, 17 September 2015

- Jammu and Kashmir 1965 (theatre honour)
- Punjab 1965 (theatre honour)
- Rajasthan 1965 (theatre honour)
- Assal Uttar
- Burki
- Dograi
- Hajipir
- Hussainiwala
- Kalidhar
- OP Hill
- Phillora

Wars

Refugees awaiting evacuation by IAF Dakota on Poonch Airstrip, December 1947.

Indo-Pakistani War of 1947

Main article: Indo-Pakistani War of 1947

Indian soldiers during the 1947–1948 war.

The war, also called the **First Kashmir War**, started in October 1947 when Pakistan feared that the Maharaja of the princely state of Kashmir and Jammu would accede to India. Following partition, princely states were left to choose whether to join India or Pakistan or to remain independent. Jammu and Kashmir, the largest of the princely states, had a majority Muslim population and significant fraction of Hindu population, all ruled by the Hindu Maharaja Hari Singh. Tribal Islamic forces with support from the army of Pakistan attacked and occupied parts of the princely state forcing the Maharaja to sign the Instrument of Accession of the princely state to the Dominion of India to receive Indian military aid. The UN Security Council passed Resolution 47 on 22 April 1948. The fronts solidified gradually along what came to be known as the Line of Control. A formal cease-fire was declared at 23:59 on the night of 1 January 1949.[9]:379 India gained control of about two-thirds of the state (Kashmir valley, Jammu and Ladakh) whereas Pakistan gained roughly a third of Kashmir (Azad Kashmir, and Gilgit–Baltistan). The Pakistan controlled areas are collectively referred to as Pakistan administered Kashmir.[10][11][12][13]

Indo-Pakistani War of 1965

Main article: Indo-Pakistani War of 1965

This war started following Pakistan's Operation Gibraltar, which was designed to infiltrate forces into Jammu and Kashmir to precipitate an insurgency against rule by India. India retaliated by launching a full-scale military attack on West Pakistan. The seventeen-day war caused thousands of casualties on both sides and witnessed the largest engagement of armored vehicles and the largest tank battle since World War II.[14][15] The hostilities between the two countries ended after a ceasefire was declared following diplomatic intervention by the Soviet Union and USA and the subsequent issuance of the Tashkent Declaration.[16] India had the upper hand over Pakistan when the ceasefire was declared.[17][18][19][20][21][22][23][24][25]

Indo-Pakistani War of 1971

Main articles: Indo-Pakistani War of 1971 and Bangladesh Liberation War

Lieutenant-General A. A. K. Niazi, the commander of Pakistan Eastern Command, signing the instrument of surrender in Dhaka on 16 Dec 1971, in the presence of India's Lt. Gen. Jagjit Singh Aurora.

Pakistan's PNS *Ghazi*, the Pakistani submarine which sank during the 1971 Indo-Pakistani War under mysterious circumstances[26] off the Visakhapatnam coast.

This war was unique in the way that it did not involve the issue of Kashmir, but was rather precipitated by the crisis created by the political battle brewing in erstwhile East Pakistan (now Bangladesh) between Sheikh Mujibur Rahman, Leader of East Pakistan, and Yahya Khan and Zulfikar Ali Bhutto, leaders of West Pakistan. This would culminate in the declaration of Independence of Bangladesh from the state system of Pakistan. Following Operation Searchlight and the 1971 Bangladesh atrocities, about 10 million Bengalis in East Pakistan took refuge in neighbouring India.[27] India intervened in the ongoing Bangladesh liberation movement.[28][29] After a large scale pre-emptive strike by Pakistan, full-scale hostilities between the two countries commenced.

Pakistan attacked at several places along India's western border with Pakistan, but the Indian Army successfully held their positions. The Indian Army quickly responded to the Pakistan Army's movements in the west and made some initial gains, including capturing around 5,795 square miles ($15,010 \text{ km}^2$)[30][31][32] of Pakistan territory (land gained by India in Pakistani Kashmir, Pakistani Punjab and Sindh sectors but gifted it back to Pakistan in the Simla Agreement of 1972, as a gesture of goodwill). Within two weeks of intense fighting, Pakistani forces in East Pakistan surrendered to the joint command of Indian and Bangladeshi forces following which the People's Republic of Bangladesh was created.[33] This war saw the highest number of casualties in any of the India-Pakistan conflicts, as well as the largest number of prisoners of war since the Second World War after the surrender of more than 90,000 Pakistani military and civilians.[34] In the words of one Pakistani author, "Pakistan lost half its navy, a quarter of its air force and a third of its army".[35]

Indo-Pakistani War of 1999

Main article: Kargil War

Commonly known as the Kargil War, this conflict between the two countries was mostly limited. During early 1999, Pakistani troops infiltrated across the Line of Control (LoC) and occupied Indian territory mostly in the Kargil district. India responded by launching a major military and diplomatic offensive to drive out the Pakistani infiltrators.[36] Two months into the conflict, Indian troops had slowly retaken most of the ridges that were encroached by the infiltrators.[37][38] According to official count, an estimated 75%–80% of the intruded area and nearly all high ground was back under Indian control.[39] Fearing large-scale escalation in military conflict, the international community, led by the United States, increased diplomatic pressure on Pakistan to withdraw forces from remaining Indian territory.[36][40] Faced with the possibility of international isolation, the already fragile Pakistani economy was weakened further.[41][42] The morale of Pakistani forces after the withdrawal declined as many units of the Northern Light Infantry suffered heavy casualties.[43][44] The government refused to accept the dead bodies of many officers,[45][46] an issue that provoked outrage and protests in the Northern Areas.[47][48] Pakistan initially did not acknowledge many of its casualties, but Nawaz Sharif later said that over 4,000 Pakistani troops were killed in the operation and that Pakistan had lost the conflict.[49][50] By the end of July 1999, organized hostilities in the Kargil district had ceased.[40] The war was a major military defeat for the Pakistani Army.[51][52]

Other armed engagements

Apart from the aforementioned wars, there have been skirmishes between the two nations from time to time. Some have bordered on all-out war, while others were limited in scope. The countries were expected to fight each other in 1955 after warlike posturing on both sides, but full-scale war did not break out.[16]

Standing armed conflicts

- Insurgency in Jammu and Kashmir: An insurgency in Kashmir has been a cause for heightened tensions. India has also accused Pakistan-backed militant groups of executing several terrorist attacks across India.
- Siachen conflict: In 1984, India launched Operation Meghdoot capturing all of the Siachen Glacier. Further clashes erupted in the glacial area in 1985, 1987 and 1995 as Pakistan sought, without success, to oust India from its stronghold.[16][53]
- Insurgency in Balochistan: An insurgency in Balochistan province of Pakistan has also caused tensions recently. Pakistan has accused India of causing the insurgency with the help of ousted Baloch leaders, militant groups and terrorist organizations like the Balochistan Liberation Army. According to Pakistani Officials these militants are trained in neighboring Afghanistan. In 2016, Pakistan alleged that an Indian spy Kulbhushan Jadhav was arrested by Pakistani forces during a counter-intelligence operation in Balochistan.[54][55]

Past skirmishes and standoffs

- Operation Brasstacks: The largest of its kind in South Asia, it was conducted by India between November 1986 and March 1987. Pakistani mobilisation in response raised tensions and fears that it could lead to another war between the two neighbours.[16]:129[56]
- 2001–2002 India–Pakistan standoff: The terrorist attack on the Indian Parliament on 13 December 2001, which India blamed on the Pakistan-based terrorist organisations, Lashkar-e-Taiba and Jaish-e-Mohammed, prompted the 2001–2002 India–Pakistan standoff and brought both sides close to war.[57]
- 2008 India Pakistan standoff: a stand-off between the two nations following the 2008 Mumbai attacks which was defused by diplomatic efforts. Following ten coordinated shooting and bombing attacks across Mumbai, India's largest city, tensions heightened between the two countries since India claimed interrogation results alleging[58][59] Pakistan's ISI supporting the attackers while Pakistan denied it.[60][61][62] Pakistan placed its air force on alert and moved troops to the Indian border, voicing concerns about proactive movements of the Indian Army[63] and the Indian government's possible plans to launch attacks on Pakistani soil.[64] The tension defused in short time and Pakistan moved its troops away from border.
- India–Pakistan border skirmishes (2016–2018): On 29 September 2016, *border skirmishes between India and Pakistan* began following reported "surgical strikes" by India against militant launch pads across the Line of Control in Pakistani-administered Kashmir "killing a large number of terrorists".[65] Pakistan rejected that a strike took place,[66] stating that Indian troops had not crossed the Line of Control but had only skirmished with Pakistani troops at the border, resulting in the deaths of two Pakistani soldiers and the wounding of nine.[67][68] Pakistan rejected India's reports of any other casualties.[69] Pakistani sources reported that at least 8 Indian soldiers were killed in the exchange, and one was captured.[70][71] India confirmed that one of its soldiers was in Pakistani custody, but denied that it was linked to the incident or that any of its soldiers had been killed.[72] The Indian operation was said to be in retaliation for a militant attack on the Indian army at Uri on 18 September in the Indian-administered state of Jammu and Kashmir that left 19 soldiers dead.[73][74] In the

succeeding days and months, India and Pakistan continued to exchange fire along the border in Kashmir, resulting in dozens of military and civilian casualties on both sides.

- 2019 India–Pakistan standoff: On 14 February 2019, a suicide attack on convoy of India's CRPF resulted in death of at least 40 troops. The responsibility of attack was claimed by Pakistan based Jaish-e-Mohammad.[75] 12 days later on February 2019, Indian jets crossed international border to conduct air strikes on alleged camp of JeM in Khyber Pakhtunkhwa province of Pakistan.[76][77] India claimed that it killed very large number of militants belonging to JeM.[78] Pakistan rejected to have suffered any losses.[79] According to the sources and satellite imagery analysis, Indian air force appears to caused minimal damage to the buildings concerned.[80][81][82][83] The incidents escalated the tension between India and Pakistan. The following day, Indian and Pakistani air forces got locked on in an aerial engagement. Pakistan claimed to have shot down two Indian aircraft and capturing one pilot Abhinandan Varthaman. Pakistan military officials claimed that the wreckage of one Indian aircraft fell in Pakistan administered Kashmir while the other one fell in Indian administered Kashmir rumored to be a Sukhoi Su-30MKI. Meanwhile Indian version was about loss a MiG-21 while shooting down a Pakistani F-16.[84] [85] The IAF also displayed remnants of an AIM-120 AMRAAM missile that they claimed could only be fired by F-16's air planes. The missiles were said to have fired against and jammed by Su-30 by IAF.[86] Pakistan rejected the Indian claim of an F-16 shot down. It initially released three or later on displayed all four air to air missiles of MiG-21 Bison with all missile seeker heads recovered intact from the wreckage however with mid-body of one of R-73 destroyed and claimed that non of missiles were ever fired.[87] Following the threats of a full scale war,[88] Abhinandan was released within two days. The Pentagon correspondent of Foreign Policy magazine, in a report claimed that Pakistan invited the United States to physically count its F-16 planes after the incident. Two senior U.S. defense officials told Foreign Policy that U.S. personnel recently counted Pakistan's F-16s and found none missing.[89] India released the electronic footage of aerial engagement to re-assert its claims.[90][91] The Pentagon rejected the magazine reports of any count ever conducted.[92] Stand off followed with intermittent firings across the LoC. Months later on 8 August, India on its air force day, flew same Su-30 "Avenger 1" in parade that was earlier being speculated to have been shot down.[93]

Incidents

- Atlantique Incident: Pakistan Navy's Naval Air Arm Breguet Atlantique patrol plane, carrying 16 people on board, was shot down by the Indian Air Force for alleged violation of airspace. The episode took place in the Rann of Kutch on 10 August 1999, just a month after the Kargil War, creating a tense atmosphere between India and Pakistan. Foreign diplomats noted that the plane fell inside Pakistani territory, although it may have crossed the border. However, they also believe that India's reaction was unjustified.[94] Pakistan later lodged a compensation claim at the International Court of Justice, accusing India for the incident, but the Court dismissed the case in a split decision ruling the Court did not have jurisdiction.[95]
- The 2011 India–Pakistan border shooting incident took place between 30 August and 1 September 2011 across the Line of Control in Kupwara District/Neelam Valley, resulting in five Indian soldiers[96] and three Pakistani soldiers being killed. Both countries gave different accounts of the incident, each accusing the other of initiating the hostilities.[97][98]
- 2013 India–Pakistan border incident in the Mendhar sector of Jammu & Kashmir, due to the beheading of an Indian soldier. A total of 22 soldiers (12 Indian and 10 Pakistani) died.[99]
- 2014–16 India–Pakistan border skirmishes in Arnia sector of Jammu & Kashmir due to killing of 1 soldier of Border Security Force and injured 3 soldiers and 4 civilians by Pakistan Rangers.[100]
- India–Pakistan border skirmishes (2016–2018)

Nuclear weapons

The nuclear conflict between both countries is of passive strategic nature with nuclear doctrine of Pakistan stating a first strike policy, although the strike would only be initiated if and only if, the Pakistan Armed Forces are unable to halt an invasion (as for example in 1971 war) or a nuclear strike is launched against Pakistan,[citation needed] whereas India has a declared policy of no first use.

- Pokhran-I (Smiling Buddha): On 18 May 1974 India detonated an 8-kiloton[101] nuclear device at Pokhran Test Range, becoming the first nation to become nuclear capable outside the five permanent members of United Nations Security Council as well as dragging Pakistan along with it into a nuclear arms race[102] with the Pakistani prime minister Zulfikar Ali Bhutto swearing to reciprocate India quoting "My countrymen would prefer having a nuclear bomb even if they have to eat grass".[103] The Pakistan Atomic Energy Commission (PAEC) Chairman Munir Ahmed Khan said that the test would force Pakistan to test its own nuclear bomb.[104]
- Kirana-I: In the 1980s a series of 24 different cold tests were conducted by PAEC, led by chairman Munir Ahmad Khan under extreme secrecy.[105] The tunnels at Kirana Hills, Sargodha, are reported to have been bored after the Chagai nuclear test sites, it is widely believed that the tunnels were constructed sometime between 1979 and 1983. As in Chagai, the tunnels at Kirana Hills had been bored and then sealed and this task was also undertaken by PAEC's DTD.[105] Later due to excessive US intelligence and satellite focus on the Kirana Hills site,[citation needed] it was abandoned and nuclear weapons testing was shifted to the Kala Chitta Range.
- Pokhran-II (Operation Shakti): On 11 May 1998 India detonated another five nuclear devices at Pokhran Test Range. With jubilation and large scale approval from the Indian society came International sanctions as a reaction to this test, the most vehement reaction of all coming from Pakistan. Great ire was raised in Pakistan, which issued a stern statement claiming that India was instigating a nuclear arms race in the region. Pakistan vowed to match India's nuclear capability with statements like: "We are in a headlong arms race on the subcontinent".[106][107]
- Chagai-I: (Youm-e-Takbir) Within half a month of Pokhran-II, on 28 May 1998 Pakistan detonated five nuclear devices to reciprocate India in the nuclear arms race. Pakistani public, like the Indian, reacted with a celebration and heightened sense of nationalism for responding to India in kind and becoming the only Muslim nuclear power. The day was later given the title Youm-e-Takbir to further proclaim such.[108][109]
- Chagai-II: Two days later, on 30 May 1998, Pakistan detonated a sixth nuclear device completing its own series of underground tests with this being the last the two nations have carried out to date.[109][110]

Annual celebrations

The nations of South Asia observe national and armed forces-specific days which originate from conflicts between India and Pakistan as follows:

- 28 May (since 1998) as Youm-e-Takbir (**The day of Greatness**) in Pakistan.[111][112]
- 26 July (since 1999) as Kargil Vijay Diwas (**Kargil Victory Day**) in India.
- 6 September (since 1965) as Defence Day (**Youm-e-Difa**) in Pakistan.[113]
- 7 September (since 1965) as Air Force Day (**Youm-e-Fizaya**) in Pakistan.[113]
- 8 September (since 1965) as Victory Day/Navy Day (**Youm-e-Bahr'ya**) in Pakistan.
- 4 December (since 1971) as Navy Day in India.
- 16 December (since 1971) as Vijay Diwas (**Victory Day**) in India.
- 16 December (since 1971) as Bijoy Dibosh (**Victory Day**) in Bangladesh.
- 29 September (since 2018) as Prakarm Parv

Involvement of other nations

- Soviet Union:

  - The USSR remained neutral during the 1965 war[114] and played a pivotal role in negotiating the peace agreement between India and Pakistan.[115]
  - The Soviet Union provided diplomatic and military assistance to India during the 1971 war. In response to the US and UK's deployment of the aircraft carriers USS *Enterprise* and HMS *Eagle*, Moscow sent nuclear submarines and warships with anti-ship missiles in the Arabian Sea and Indian Ocean, respectively.[116][117][118]

- United States:

  - The US had not given any military aid to Pakistan in the Indo-Pakistani War of 1965.[119]
  - The United States provided diplomatic and military support to Pakistan during the 1971 war by sending USS *Enterprise* into the Indian Ocean.[120][121][122]
  - The United States did not support Pakistan during the Kargil War, and successfully pressured the Pakistani administration to end hostilities.[36][123][124]

- China:

  - China had helped Pakistan in various wars with diplomatic support.[18][125][126]

- Russia:

  - Russia maintained a non-belligerent policy for both sides. Russia helped negotiate peace in 2001–02 and helped divert the 2008 crisis.[127][128]

In popular culture

These wars have provided source material for both Indian and Pakistani film and television dramatists, who have adapted events of the war for the purposes of drama and to please target audiences in their nations.

Indian films

- *Hindustan Ki Kasam*, a 1973 Hindi war film based on Operation Cactus Lilly of the 1971 Indo-Pakistani War, directed by Chetan Anand.
- *Aakraman*, a 1975 Hindi war film based on the 1971 Indo-Pakistan war, directed by I. Om Prakash.
- *Vijeta*, a 1982 Hindi film based on the 1971 Indo-Pakistan war, produced by Shashi Kapoor and directed by Govind Nihalani.
- *Param Vir Chakra*, a 1995 Hindi film based on Indo-Pakistani War, directed by Ashok Kaul.[129]
- *Border*, a 1997 Hindi war film based on the Battle of Longewala of the 1971 Indo-Pakistan war, directed by J.P.Dutta.
- *LOC Kargil*, a 2003 Hindi war film based on the Kargil War, directed by J. P. Dutta.
- *Deewaar*, a 2004 Hindi film starring Amitabh Bachchan based on the POW of the 1971 Indo-Pakistan war, directed by Milan Luthria.

- *Lakshya*, a 2004 Hindi film partially based on the events of the Kargil War, directed by Farhan Akhtar.
- *1971*, 2007 Hindi war film based on a true story of prisoners of war after the Indo-Pakistani war of 1971, directed by Amrit Sagar.
- *Kurukshetra*, a 2008 Malayalam film starring Mohanlal based on Kargil War, directed by Major Ravi.
- *Tango Charlie*, a 2005 Hindi film starring Ajay Devgan, and Bobby Deol based on Kargil Conflict, directed by Mani Shankar.
- *The Ghazi Attack*, a 2017 Telugu and Hindi bilingual film based on the sinking of *PNS Ghazi*.
- *1971: Beyond Borders*, a 2017 Malayalam film, directed by Major Ravi.
- *Raazi*, a 2018 Hindi film about an Indian spy during the Indo Pakistan war of 1971, directed by Meghna Gulzar
- *Uri: The Surgical Strike*, a 2019 Hindi film about India's surgical strike into the Pakistani base camps after the Uri incident in 2016.

Pakistani films, miniseries and dramas

- *Angaar Waadi*, an Urdu drama serial based on the Kashmir conflict, directed by Rauf Khalid[130]
- *Laag*, an Urdu drama serial based on the Kashmir conflict, directed by Rauf Khalid[130]
- *PNS Ghazi (Shaheed)*, an Urdu drama based on sinking of PNS Ghazi, ISPR
- *Alpha Bravo Charlie*, an Urdu drama serial based on three different aspects of Pakistan Army's involvement in action, directed by Shoaib Mansoor
- *Sipahi Maqbool Hussain*, an Urdu drama serial based on a 1965 war POW, directed by Haider Imam Rizvi

AUTHOR BIO

AUTHOR BIO

MY NAME IS VIVEK KUMAR PANDEY . I WAS BORN IN 30 SEP 2002,I AM FROM SURAT GUJARAT INDIA.MY DREAM WAS TO BE GOOD WRITERS ,MY FAMILY SUPPORTED ME TO SUCCESSFUL AND I CAN DO IT MY SELF.How do I write? That is a question, I believe, that cannot be honestly answered by me."CELEBRATING YOUNGST WRITER AWARD WINNER IN GUJARAT 1ST RANK". I may think I did a good job writing something when in reality it could be horrible. The reader is the one who decides the quality of my writing. I do not find writing to be natural to me and therefore find it to be a real challenge. My trick as a challenged writer is to do the best I can and know that I am happy with the final outcome. It may take a while to do my best and there may be quite a few problems I run into along the way.

When I write I come across a few problems that always tend to slow me down. Finding the right words is the hardest part. While I write, I try to picture what words will follow the writing I have already completed. I can rarely find the words I want or make my writing sound the way I would like it to. When I first started writing my main problem was, and still is, writer's block. I've learned to overcome that by coming up with every way I can to say what is in my head and put it on paper. It may not always work how I would like it to but it allows me to state my mind to the best of my abilities. In the end it is all about getting what is in your head onto the paper. That is one of the main factors that can affect my opinion of my writing. how to i am become a writer ,there is support of my family and teachers now i am become a writer.my fav sports is cricket and i like summer season etc.in class 5th i started writing like poem and story other.you can do everything and do it 's your self."THOSE WHO TRY NEVER GIVE UP".

In order for me to have a good opinion of my writing I have to like what I am writing about. If I am not interested in the topic I am writing about I will get bored of it and my disinterest will be obvious in the end result. I enjoy being able to state my opinion and write how I feel. My best work is on a topic I enjoy and includes what I think and feel about it. From past and recent experiences I have learned that I am more proud of work I have enjoyed writing and researching for. In the past I have enjoyed writing short stories and assignments on subjects that intrigue me or are on some of my personal interests. In the end I believe it my self.............

MR VIVEK KUMAR PANDEY SHAMBHUNATH PUBLISHED 50+BOOK